WHISPERING
THE DRAGON

Shamanic Techniques
to Awaken Your Primal Power

Lujan Matus

Disclaimer

All rights reserved. No part of this publication may be reproduced or transferred in any form or by any means, graphic, electronic, or mechanical, including photocopying, recording, taping, or by any information storage retrieval system, without the written permission of the author. The author specifically disclaims any responsibility for any liability, loss, or risk, personal or otherwise, which is incurred as a consequence, directly or indirectly, of the use and application of any of the contents of this book.

© Copyright 2014 Lujan Matus.

All poetry by Lujan Matus unless otherwise indicated.

The Parallel Perception logo is copyright. No unauthorized use.

ISBN-10: 1499525613

ISBN-13: 9781499525618

Dedication

Thank you to all who contributed to the proof reading, your time and care is greatly appreciated.

Special thanks to my beautiful wife, Mizpah Matus.

Acknowledgements

Cover art by Grinning Tree.

Editing, formatting, cover design layout and back cover synopsis by Naomi Jean.

TABLE OF CONTENTS

FOREWORD I

THE EIGHT GATES OF DREAMING AWAKE 1

THE ORIGIN OF SIN 5

LOOK AT WHAT YOU CAN'T SEE 19

LISTEN TO WHAT YOU CAN'T HEAR 32

INNER SILENCE 45

THE MEDICINE WHEEL OF WISDOM 54

BEING, KNOWING, AND DOING 60

THE ART OF BEING, KNOWING,
AND NOT-DOING 79

THE BULLET HAS ONLY ONE GUN 89

SEEKING VALIDATION 98

BARDO 107

PERSONAL POWER 120

ADVANCED RECAPITULATION 130

LISTENING POWER 148

GESTURES OF SPIRIT 164

THE LAST SEVEN GATES 174

YOUR PHOTONIC POTENTIAL 191

SEEING 194

EIGHT GATES SUMMARY 197

GENERAL ESOTERICS 203

THE MICROCOSMIC ORBIT 213

GLOSSARY 219

Foreword

This book will challenge you to release your social persona in exchange for your most powerful primal self. Your journey through the *Eight Gates* will awaken you specifically in the areas that you need to address in order to arrive upon your own omnipresence.

We are all subject to the social programming that was introduced to us in early childhood and which inevitably manifests its limitation throughout our lifetime. We become conditionally habituated into that inherited mindset so completely that we accept its reach, abilities and methodology as all that is available to us.

Within these pages we will discover that this apparent coherency we have been indoctrinated into is not as such. The wisdom, authentic self and freedom we seek exist outside the boundaries of that social dilemma.

Einstein famously stated that a problem cannot be solved on the same level of consciousness that created it. The techniques Lujan shares will prompt you to go beyond your conditioning to discover the wisdom that lies deep within.

Within the human biofield, entry points or gates can be located. They are formless, yet will attain form through applying the exercises contained within this extraordinary book.

This is an age-old journey and Lujan offers a practical path, through the *Eight Gates of Dreaming Awake*, beyond programmed limitations and into a vaster, more fulfilling experience of self.

FOREWORD

Read this text for guidance and apply the techniques until you awaken to what was always there. Persevere until the silence speaks where your chattering mind once claimed false domain.

Your destination is a place with great depth that has always been there. Passing through the formless thresholds of the *Eight Gates of Dreaming Awake*, you will learn to observe what can't be seen, obtain the feelings of that which cannot be touched and listen to what can't be heard.

Welcome to the most important journey you will ever embark upon.

The Eight Gates of Dreaming Awake

The Eight Gates are portals within our biosphere that we inwardly traverse so as to awaken ourselves to the deeper wisdom that resides within our body consciousness. The journey you are about to embark upon will change your life completely.

Entering the *Eight Gates* will facilitate a momentary pause within the habitual social narrative that you have been entrained to accept as a substitute for your sovereign self.

Interrupting the continuity of this programming is crucial in order to realize that we are more than what we have been taught to believe.

The quietude achieved by practicing the *Eight Gates* will allow deep inner silence to radiate throughout your entire being, bringing peace and happiness within, and awakening your internal seer to bear witness to your present reality.

I would like to invite you now into the *Eight Gates*. The majority of this book is dedicated to the first gate, for it is the most complex and pivotal threshold that one can ever encounter. It stands in complete opposition to the social moorings that we have been subject to since the moment of conception, and must be crossed in order to reclaim one's personal power.

Upon entering the first gate, we will be faced with three initial elements that we must become aware of. We will traverse each of these in sequence to bring about a deeper understanding of their essential nature, and this process will propagate one of the most sought after states on the warrior's path: inner silence.

With these techniques we're going to reverse your eyes, reverse your ears, and instruct you on how to anchor these primordial elements symbiotically within that quietude.

Once your awareness has been inwardly restored, you will begin to realize that there is form within emptiness and emptiness within form.

When this very subtle parameter is established, a primal base of operations will automatically become available to you, in comparison to the pressing matters that you encounter on your personal journey. Now let's examine all the elements that may confront you on this path.

If you do not change direction,

you may end up where you are heading.

Lao Tzu

The Origin of Sin

The word *sin*, in one of its original forms, means to not be absolutely present, to miss the point, or to be absently available. Original sin is an element that is introduced to us during early childhood, before we can actually think or recognize the phenomenon known as thought within our minds.

Our childhood origins were excitable, joyful, and absolutely exuberant; we were composed of these buoyant feelings and nothing else. For everybody there existed this original state of purity and happiness, where we were not subject to any form of corruption.

What I want to do now is ask you a question. Can you remember a time in your childhood when somebody walked into the room and they filled you with joy? Do you recall that sensation arriving within your body?

This recollection doesn't need to be precise. It only has to be strong enough within you to remind you of that experience.

Remember being empty and clear, and as that person entered your environment you were truly filled with joy and happiness. You felt very secure when they arrived. Recall that you didn't think about knowing what that person brought into the room with their presence, you simply recognized them as they appeared.

As you saw them, your body was filled with the knowledge that this person was truly there for you. You knew without thought. You didn't have to think about it, and actually you weren't thinking at all, at that particular stage.

Now I want you to recall another time where someone walked into your childhood memory and you felt that they were threatening. You weren't comfortable with them and their mere presence created fear inside your body.

Remember an occasion like that. Again, it doesn't have to be a detailed recollection. Just know it, remember it, and recognize that you did have these feelings as a result of that person's presence.

What I want you to realize is that the experience occurred without thought. There is no syntactical process, in terms of your mind talking to itself, taking place. This is your body recognizing something that is inside that person, which has momentarily entered you.

What we're actually looking at here is how that person was you, and how you recognize them because you see that person within yourself, with your inner sight. You virtually become them at that point, but in the same breath, you are not them.

For you as a child, at that stage of your development,

there was no discernable separation between you and them, by virtue of the fact that you had not developed the clear boundaries that define your inner sight in comparison to the aggressive input of another. What we are going to examine is how you were coercively manipulated away from these pure experiences very early on.

Through the practice of the *Eight Gates* we will establish a base of operations for your personal power to flourish so that you will be able to distinguish where your boundary is in comparison to that which has entered within your childhood, and which has had overriding consequences within your adult life.

Now let's get back to the original sin, in terms of a promise that was given to you; the first promise that was also the first lie. The first lie is a really important element to be examined, for it leads on to fundamental future ramifications in your life.

When you realize that you were lied to, the roots of this deception will inevitably turn into resentment and a sense of entitlement. Resentment and entitlement develop into a whole host of other recognizable traits as one grows older.

As we go through this process, you'll begin to realize that these characteristics are apparent in almost everybody that you meet. What I want to do next is use some word associations.

When you felt these people come into the room, you had a feeling within your chest. Let's call this feeling *presence*. These feelings awakened within you a certain perception, which actually was your presence, for you became aware of them and so their presence became alive inside you. *Presence* is the first term that we're going to use in terms of this word association.

When you were small, one of the original coercive manipulations was applied around Christmas time, when you were told the first lie: That Santa Claus was going to bring you a present, but you had to be good. This was one of the earliest blackmails that you were ever subject to. Be good and you'll get these presents.

You believed that there was such a thing as Santa Claus.

This is the first lie, and you were very happy about that deception. Your parents were openly transparent about giving you that story as if it were real, but you didn't realize that it was actually false. So, you excitedly go to bed the night before Christmas thinking, "There's a present under the tree."

Here we have the two words: The external *presents* that were conditionally promised to you and the internal *presence*, that we discussed as a feeling that you have inside yourself.

Now, remember that you're in your bed and you have the visualization of the presents alive and vibrant in your awareness. This visualization takes you to the box under the tree, which is a present that has been put there by a false entity, a false character.

Even though the gifts were probably under the tree three weeks before Christmas, you didn't question the fact that this guy was supposed to come down the chimney the night before and give it to you.

There were a lot of inconsistencies within this lie. These disparities lay the basic groundwork that sets up feelings of insecurity that will manifest as dysfunctional behavioral patterns in the future.

Let's proceed to the next word association. The person who was supposed to be delivering this present, who was fulfilling your wishes and your dreams, if you were good, his name was Santa Claus. I want you to look at the second word, *Claus*. Though it's spelled as *Claus*, I want you to see it as *claws,* as in the claws of a feline.

The claws are there to scratch you, or keep you away if you are conscious of the warning, but at this stage you are a child, and unaware. Your seeing is not mature enough to recognize the *claws*. Cats are well known for killing birds, even though they have a full stomach.

The very nature of these claws is that if you are in their vicinity they will ensnare and take away the innocence of that song being sung of itself within its purity. But in this particular case they're dangerous for you in terms of threatening punishment; specifically by withholding something you want.

This withholding breeds greed and desire as an inserted

malaise applied to the innocence that has already been stolen through your internal song, which is your silence, being disrupted by this program.

Let's examine another meaning to be found here, the *clause* at the bottom of documents, where the small print is written. If you don't read the clause and you're not aware about what you're assigning your signature to, that fine print could be a trick or a trap that may ensnare you.

If you're not careful, the clause can imprison you through not being conscious of the ramifications that are embedded within the agreement. This is the binding effect of the original sin; not being absolutely present within the moment that you are assigning your attention to.

Now you have the fantasy of Santa Claus, and you have the reality of the physical presents that have been introduced to your attention.

Be aware that these are only word associations to give gravity to the effects of what you learn to sustain through the application of unwholesome emotional bonding via mind chatter. The true significance of the original sin is that you have been taken off point. You have been trained to assign your awareness to an illusion.

If these particular associations don't apply to your life, look carefully for your own original lie, the first sin that was applied to your perception to mislead you away from your silent reservoir of knowing.

At this point it is applicable to mention that another facet of the word sin is to be outside of one's integrity. This corresponds to the state of being held prisoner within somebody else's constructed illusion, devised to entrap you within an idea, which then becomes the false truth of your childhood reality.

Such premises are pressed upon us in childhood from our loved ones, who are repeating a script that has no real destination and thereby only finds conclusion through its repetitious nature, year after year. Even though it seems to have its origins in the idea of perpetuating a loving reality, the deceptive loop is truly Machiavellian by nature.

A crooked smile reveals a crooked path, and a crooked mind that leans upon a bent and crooked staff. From whence you came, a crooked eye reveals its crooked aim, the crooked wish to make you just the same.

THE ORIGIN OF SIN

When you are a three-year-old and you get a present, you're very happy to receive it, but this excitement only lasts for a certain amount of time. The gift is valuable for only as long as you're interested in it.

As your presence leaves your body, or the feeling of excitement that you have inside you diminishes, it gravitates towards this external value that you've begun to learn to focus on. When you're focusing on that, you're redirecting your eyes away from your body consciousness.

Would you be happy about getting the same present that you were given when you were two years old when you are four years old? Of course not! If you receive the same present as you did when you were two, it won't really suit you when you are six or seven.

The expectancy system is being instilled as a sense of entitlement; that you need to get what you want to keep you interested and excited.

You know that something that you are given as a three-year-old is not going to serve you when you're six years old because you'll be bored with it. Your entitlement tells you that you'll not be happy with that. This is how unwholesome expectation builds even before you realize that Santa Claus was a lie.

Without even knowing that you have been duped, your entitlement begins to overshadow the feeling of joy that you originally had inside yourself. As the years go by, you begin to expect and you begin to visualize what you want that's outside of yourself.

This is how we all became externalized. These instilled desires and expectations take you beyond what you need to know in your present circumstances, and thus divert you and everybody else off their life path through that conditioning.

Childhood programming will inevitably translate into distorted behavioral patterns within one's adult life, as unreasonable emotional states that will ripen and eventually equate to control issues such as entitlement and the need to be absolutely right at every turn. Understanding the roots of this conundrum is the first step towards resolving it.

Be within your heart.

See and feel with your heart.

Recognize your heart within another.

Speak words from the heart.

Receive the words of another,

within those precious chambers.

Look at What You Can't See

One of the primary applications of the original sin is the redirection of one's eyes away from the heart center, or one's true path. What we need to do now is to help you discover this truth, whereby convincing you that your eyes have been socially entrained to focus in the wrong direction.

What I'd like to ask you is this: If you gaze around you, what percentage of your focus would you give to an object, from one to a hundred? How much of your eyes would you allocate to it?

LOOK AT WHAT YOU CAN'T SEE

When you walk into a room and you see a broom, you know exactly what a broom looks like. Let's say you give any object fifty percent of your attention. Do you need to apply that much of your focus, when you recognize it at first glance?

If you see a door handle, you know exactly what it looks like and what it is. There are enormous amounts of different types of door handles, but once you see one, you don't need to utilize fifty percent of your attention to recognize its shape and function.

When you look at a tree, do you think you need to give fifty percent of your eyes to a tree? Even if you see a leaf that's fallen on the ground, and every leaf has a different shape, would you not recognize it immediately, though its form is different from the one you saw the day before?

Would you need to give fifty percent of your eyes to that? It's just a leaf. You don't need to study the obvious contours that are instantly available. In other words, the process is automatic.

What I'm going to suggest is that you give only cursory

glances to everything. Give only two percent of your eyes to the world. I want you to realize and understand that as a result of your presence being relocated outside of yourself, you give too much of your eyes to the external world and not enough of your eyes internally: to yourself and to your heart center.

Turning that gaze back is refocusing your eyes internally, but not in a selfish way. This technique will deliver you into a space of gratitude and fulfillment, for everything that you gaze upon leaves an indelible impression within that leads you to truly appreciate the very life that you live.

I'm going to convince your body and eyes now that the power of their seeing is connected not only to sight but also to feeling.

Remember that childhood state of being, when someone walks into the room and you recognize what they bring in terms of their real presence as a human being. They enter the space and you feel truly happy, even though you've only given them a cursory glance.

If you remember, as a child, you would just look up for a

moment to see them. As you glanced at them, you had all this information that arrived inside of you, as a mysterious rapture or as a strange devastation, which presented to you immediate knowing about who they were for you.

You really only gave them a cursory glance, yet, as you remember this scene, you know that it was all taking place inside you, in terms of the feelings or emotions that were produced. Everything was happening internally.

Even though these encounters are vibrantly animated within your childhood memories, such experiences will continue until the end of your days, for as we know we can't control the intentions or the actions of others. What you will learn in this book is what not to do in order to discover your primal self. But let's get back to the subject at hand.

The way that I'll demonstrate this process to you is to give you an example to show you how your eyes really work and to enable you to revoke the visual externalization that you have been indoctrinated into.

I'm going to teach you how to reverse the external

momentum of the eyes by revealing how to gaze within, in two steps. You will learn how to give ninety-eight percent of your eyes to yourself and only two percent, or a cursory glance, to the world around you.

Follow this instruction carefully. I'd like you to raise your hands up in front of you and hold them a little bit more than two feet apart, so that you have your palms turned in at a 45° angle, facing towards your eyes. Place them wide enough so that you engage your eyes peripherally, a little higher than your ears.

Now I want you to give a hard gaze to an object in front of you. Even though your eyes are immovable, upon what is directly before them, this focus will absorb only two percent of your attention. What I'd like you to do is keep your eyes locked in this position and begin to lower your hands, very, very slowly.

I want you to maintain the attention of your eyes peripherally on your hands as they gradually descend, while you keep that hard gaze locked before you, which represents only two percent of your attention.

As you're lowering your hands, I'll pre-empt what's happening to your body. You begin to feel the feeling inside your hands. As they descend, the feeling becomes stronger.

The chi emanates more powerfully. The electricity in your hands becomes really obvious. You experience the heaviness of the blood flowing into them and what accompanies this is an abundance of feeling, a contained arrival.

Now you have your peripheral gaze on your hands and you have your hard gaze, which is unwaveringly focused on whatever object you have chosen and is in actuality only a cursory glance – two percent application - in terms of the focus of your attention.

While you're looking at what appears before you, you are actually watching your hands peripherally. As you're observing your hands, you realize that your eyes have the function of feeling. You're watching the feeling inside your hands. Your eyes are now retracing their true origins back to your body.

LOOK AT WHAT YOU CAN'T SEE

Now I'd like you to do the same thing once again. This time I'd like you to hold your hands up in exactly the same position, look with the cursory glance, which appears to be a hard gaze, then close your eyes.

As you close your eyes, watch your hands with the feelings that you obtain from within while they drop slowly, in exactly the same fashion. Keep your eyes closed.

I want you to see your hands while the feeling of your eyes descends harmoniously within the act of observing them internally.

Forget about the cursory glance now and just watch the feeling of your hands as they go down, following them with your eyes shut. Even though you can't see your hands, you have a very strong sensation arriving. There is an enormous connectivity between your eyes and the feeling of your hands as they drop.

Your eyes are now ninety-eight percent watching the feeling and the flow of the chi, the energy, and the tingling arriving into your hands. They are internally viewing the sensations more strongly than the object outside of you that you were previously gazing at.

Before we go any further with this reversal, I'd like to draw your attention to something that occurred that you may have not noticed. When you were focusing on your hands while your eyes were closed, your internal gaze began to naturally follow the movement of their descent.

This is an automatic and instinctive process of your eyes. You can't control their movement. They instinctively adapt to what they can't see.

This is one of the first steps to becoming aware of intangibly touching the contours of what you can't see, in terms of all the information contained within that observation. In the beginning it may be noted as simply a feeling of what you can't see, but as you progress this will evolve into something more palpable.

These techniques are the preliminary tools that are applied in the advanced practice of recapitulation.

LOOK AT WHAT YOU CAN'T SEE

Through this process, your eyes are being subject to their full reversal in terms of correctly observing the world from within. Instead of your eyes giving fifty percent of your visual focus externally (and some people give seventy-five percent, others as much as eighty percent) we've reduced that to two percent of your attention on the world that surrounds you.

Now you have your eyes closed and your two percent has spread peripherally. It is all around you. It's only two percent, but this fraction of your attention is so powerful, by virtue of the fact that it is connected to the ninety-eight percent that's actually following the chi and the feeling inside your hands and body.

You're watching your physical being. The two-percent gaze spreads to your whole environment in an intangible way. You become more connected to your external world with your two-percent gaze while you're internally watching with the ninety-eight percent that is the feeling in your body.

Realize that your eyes were moving as if they were actually watching your hands as they dropped. There was something else that you may have overlooked that I am going to ask you to observe, to allow you to remember what you were absorbing with this cursory glance, which is still active even though your eyes are closed.

Your eyes, whilst they were in the midst of the act of watching your hands, were simultaneously viewing the ever-present memory that your body is contained within, which is your immediate environment. They are watching your recollection, the items that surround you, whether you be in a room or a rainforest.

As your eyes perform this act, they begin to extend from themselves fibers or roots that emanate from one's entire being. This is the first step to reactivating the full spectrum of your primal connectivity.

These self-aware light filaments can extend up to a hundred miles and beyond, depending on the power of the seer, and feel like internally connected, activated nerve-endings conducting the essence of everything in the environment towards one's center. An awakened intuitive empath can travel, linearly and inter-dimensionally, via this impersonal conductivity.

This first practice of the *Eight Gates*, in so doing by reversing our eyes, opens the first portal to one's present moment that is continually escaping us, and to one's inevitable future, thus in turn giving access to the content of everything that was and is, allowing the seer primal right of entry to all interdimensional continuums.

Activating this primal function is one of the hidden *not-doings* of the *Eight Gates of Dreaming Awake*, which is also known as the ancient Oriental art of *Ting Jing*. In this book I will reveal the secrets of this esoteric principle, which have not yet been fully disclosed. All I'm showing you is what you've forgotten. I'm only reminding you how to remember what you used to know, before you began thinking.

Now you know that your eyes are primarily anchored in your body first, before they see the world outside. This is the way you were when you were a child. Seeing in this way is one of the essential functions of your eyes and now that this knowing has been returned to you, you will never forget it again.

Form is within emptiness and

Emptiness is within form

Listen to What You Can't Hear

Now I want to ask you a question: What is it that you have listened to all your life that you have never heard? You've been paying attention to this one element since you were very young, even though you have never actually heard it. You've been witness to it, inside your mind. It is your internal dialogue. As you're subject to that incessant narrative, what happened to your ears?

We just looked at what happened to your eyes and how

they were redirected through the transferal of a false promise, which took your presence outside of yourself to the presents that were under a tree.

You were coercively maneuvered throughout your life to actually externalize your eyes to such a degree that you lose the sense of yourself. Not only do you lose your primal self-awareness, your inner sense has been diverted with false promises and real lies. Now you know that, your eyes can be redirected internally.

While you listen to someone, if you sense your own body, you're actually witnessing the person within yourself as you hear their voice. As you speak, I'm watching you through listening to my own inner silence.

While I'm observing myself, ninety-eight percent of my attention is on my own body. So if you do something or display a gesture, I'll become aware of it. That's the way we instinctively function, the way we operate as children.

This is how seers and shamans apply their *not-doings*. You just have to know exactly what to do with your eyes.

LISTEN TO WHAT YOU CAN'T HEAR

Without instruction it's very difficult to know what not to do in the beginning. We're going back to the original *not-doings* that were our true functioning as human beings.

You know now that the only thing you've listened to all your life that you've never heard is your internal dialogue. When you listen to the world, what percentage of your attention, from one to a hundred, would you say you give to the sounds around you?

What I'm going to suggest, which I will be able to show you, is that your ears are meant to be used one-hundred percent externally, never inwardly for listening to your internal chatter.

If you listen to the voice inside your head, your ears have been commandeered by that dialogue, which is a direct reflection of all the external items gathered internally as reactive emotions.

These placements are a result of the redirection of your attention, in terms of the possessiveness that you obtained through incorrectly diverting your own presence outside of yourself.

If you're listening to that possessive internal talk that has been swayed by distorted emotions, and you give seventy-five percent of your attention to that 'private' narrative — which is obviously revolving around the unresolved emotions that were obtained within your childhood — you are no longer listening to the world around you.

Now, if you walk into the rain forest and you're looking outwardly without looking inwardly, and you're listening to yourself speaking, could you imagine how long you would survive? Not very long. You'll be eaten very quickly, since you're not functioning as a primal being. What you're doing is operating as a social entity.

If you go into the rain forest, and you're thinking and watching the world in the normal way that you would in the suburbs, you would sit on an ants' nest and get stung, or be bitten by a snake, or eaten by a tiger, one or the other. When your primal attention has been diverted into being a socialite, you lose the awareness of your intangible self and your surroundings.

What we have to examine is that the *not-doing* of our eyes is to watch ourselves instead of watching the world around us, and to realize that the true function of our eyes is to feel what we can see. And the true function of our ears is to listen to what we've never heard.

You were taught to talk to yourself. It's practically impossible to go back and remember what was the first word you ever said inside your own head. You can't access that memory. It's equally difficult to return to that point to discover when your eyes were redirected outside your body into external layers that were inadvertently interlaced with lies and coercive maneuvers.

These limited points of reference set up your own personal resentments and entitlements, which become a myriad of problems as you mature. It becomes extremely complex to recall the non-invasiveness of the silence that has been overladen.

Examples will be given so that you can understand how it

all began and so you can begin to stop what happened. Whatever did take place, it is actually none of your business anymore. It's just a matter of realizing that it never was any of your business anyway, and then turning it around into the *not-doing* of those events.

If you make it your mission to find out exactly how you were coercively maneuvered, then you're basically remembering or recapitulating in the wrong way, for maybe you will use your self-importance to get there, and that is a misguided tactic. It's a *doing*. These doings will be explained in more depth later on.

In the previous chapter we examined the function of your eyes and reversing your eyes. Now we're going to observe the function and the reversal of your ears.

We looked at the issue of listening to what you've never heard, which is a doing, and that doing is your internal dialogue. It's a very strong doing. It's the strongest doing that divided you, in terms of splitting your attention.

This is the split-tongue principle. Once you begin to talk

to yourself, you no longer listen to your heart, thus splitting yourself in two. You have your one true voice, which erupts from your heart, and the other voice that incessantly talks to you inside your head. As this division occurs between your head and your heart, an ocean of poison begins to separate you from yourself.

This is the essence of the story of the exodus from the Garden of Eden, which is the exile from one's truth and innocence. The metaphor of the serpent is supplied to give concrete value to the notion that, even though you have bitten into the supposed wisdom, you have been inadvertently poisoned through taking that bite, and your exodus from your own inner silence is the result.

The sensory overload of the false voice gives rise to the chasm that splits one's perception in two, thus leading one away from one's true insights and wholeness, by providing a surrogate self that substitutes your wisdom with a constantly nagging internal dialogue.

What I will now reveal to you is a technique to free you

from this insidious phenomenon. I'm going to ask you to listen to what you can't hear. When you listen to what you can't hear, something very magical will happen. You'll know immediately how to turn off your internal talk.

One of the biggest issues with almost everyone on the warrior's path is the inability to shut down their internal dialogue. Some may have been studying shamanism all their life, perhaps for thirty or forty years, or sometimes even longer, yet the most common problem still arises. They can't stop that incessant voice.

We're going to review the practical aspects of traversing the first gate over and over again, in different ways, so as to obtain a deeper understanding of this ancient entry point to true shamanism.

What we're doing is introducing you to real *not-doings*. Not tying your shoelace a different way, not putting your belt on backwards, not walking backwards. These are not *not-doings*. These are just *doings* turned around to look like *not-doings*.

Reversing your eyes is a real *not-doing*. Reversing your ears is another. What we're going to do now is give you a technique so that you can stop your internal dialogue. Once you know how to do this, you can never say you don't know how to shut it down.

You can use the next technique, and all the others that I'm giving you, for the rest of your life to release yourself from that incessant internal nagging.

I'd like you to take a loud breath in, and then breathe out, loudly. Now you know where your breath is. But that didn't work, did it? You're still thinking. Your ears weren't redirected.

What I would now like to impart is the true function of the breath in terms of its esoteric value, and this technique will anchor your eyes within. As the breath internally establishes itself through this method, it will also anchor your ears externally. It's what you do with your breath and what you don't do with your breath that makes it a *not-doing*.

It's vitally important to understand what you don't do. When you understand what you're not going to do with your breath, then your ears and your eyes will be naturally anchored in their correct position.

As you begin this exercise, listen to the sounds that are around you so that you can see what happens. What I want you to do is to take a breath in and out, so quietly that you can't hear it. I want you to close your eyes so that you're watching your body as well. When you breathe so quietly that you can't hear it, I want you to attempt to listen to what you can't hear.

As you breathe in and out, this rhythm is inaudible, for you've done it so quietly. Allow your ears to listen to what they can't hear.

When you realize you can't hear your silent breath, what happens to your auditory function? You began to recognize that you could hear the birds outside very clearly. When you listen to what you can't hear, what else happens? You can't think.

When you listen to what you can't hear, you begin to notice everything outside of you, auditorily. Then you begin to see your silence, and listen to it.

Listen to what you can't hear. As you immerse yourself in this attention your internal dialogue turns off. Instead of listening to that incessant internal talk, now you're listening to what you can't hear. When you listen to what you can't hear, your ears become externalized, one hundred percent.

Your eyes now are ninety-eight percent looking at your body. You're anchoring this with your silent breath. You're now using your eyes ninety-eight percent to view yourself internally, while your two percent cursory glance is gently perusing the world around you.

You're watching your feelings and you're feeling them more strongly, by virtue of the fact that you're watching them. You realize that your eyes are symbiotically connected to these feelings.

By being aware of your feelings, you're actually looking at what you can't see. When you listen to what you can't hear, you've located the position inside your body where you can observe your inner silence. When you discover that you can look at what you can't feel and listen to what you can't hear through anchoring yourself with your silent breath, you've found a space of inner silence in your body.

When you arrive upon this reservoir, it's intangible. When you look at your feelings, they are there, but they are invisible to you. Yet you witness them. Thus you have arrived within the sanctuary of the first gate. When you listen to what you can't hear, you are delivered into your heart center.

The quieter you become,

the more you are able to hear.

Lao Tzu

Inner Silence

When you listen to what you can't hear, you begin to hear all the sounds outside of you. When you begin to look at what you can't see, you start to feel everything inside your body. You're alerted to the sounds outside of you by virtue of being focused on nothing; which is your internal emptiness within.

When you focus on this *not-doing* you become aware, by looking at your body, that you can actually feel the sounds that are outside of you. You can see those sounds, for your eyes are automatically directed to look where you don't expect, and then you may obtain what you shouldn't reasonably know.

You will receive the unexpected by virtue of that act. Look back and remember the natural reflex of that cursory glance that delivers information pertinent to your internal capacity to absorb what presents itself.

I want everybody to be aware that this is not an easy subject. It is the beginning of the end of the social self, and of substantially becoming aware of the hidden knowing, as a *not-doing* of the constructed reinforced reality that we are subject to twenty-four seven.

You're looking at your inner silence. You're listening to your inner silence. You're feeling your inner silence. You've located it in the center of your being. When you identify it, it spreads harmoniously to the four corners of your physical body.

You become very comfortable and very peaceful since you're no longer talking to yourself. You're actually doing what you are meant to be doing as a shaman and what you did originally as a child.

Within those gestures, listening to what you can't hear, looking at what you can't see, and feeling what you can't touch, everything becomes available, by virtue of the fact that the essence of all things emanates from its eternal central matrix as a frequency.

Everything is bound by that rule, for this inaudible phenomenon reveals itself to you as feelings that you can't touch, and vibrations that appear as your words. Even though they are not heard they are spoken.

These are the *not-doing*s of your eyes and your ears, which are actually the most primal *not-doing*s that will deliver you into a true empathic state that is honestly invisible to itself as it appears.

Upon your arrival, these *not-doing*s beckon the inner silence that gathers you into the essence of yourself, which becomes the feelings that you traverse upon as your inaudible wisdom.

INNER SILENCE

When you look and you listen, you are hearing everything that is being said. And equally when you speak you are listening to everything that is voiced, since it's not connected to any form of thought process.

Now let's connect all these dots and make these *not-doing*s functional for you. What I need you to realize is that the only things of importance that you have in your life are the experiences that you encounter. There's nothing that you can obtain beyond your own experiences. We just need to put this collage together in a way that can be understood, without forcing that understanding.

Once you have located this point of inner silence then you can begin to gather that quietude by intently focusing upon it.

When you listen to what you can't hear, you locate that point of silence inside yourself, and you identify everything outside by virtue of focusing inwardly. You become aware. You make contact with that silent reservoir while you listen to what you can't hear.

INNER SILENCE

As you focus internally, you become acutely conscious of and attuned to the sounds around you. When you focus your eyes inside your body, in terms of watching yourself and the feelings you obtain, you're absorbing those sensations and impressions and only giving cursory glances to the world around you.

You're fully active and fully awake. When you do this, then you become aware of where your inner silence is located, even though it is non-locatable.

A lot of people don't know how to become silent for they are continually talking to themselves. They're listening to what they have never heard. If you are listening to your internal dialogue, your original voice from your heart has been split into two by being partially relocated within your mind.

Your heart has only one voice and it arises from within as you speak. As you have spoken, you listen to what you're saying. You don't script and talk to yourself about what you're going to say.

You just give voice to what needs to be said, and in your

body what arrives is as much of a surprise for you as for everybody else. There's really no truth in a scripted gem. They're a dime a dozen.

Now you know exactly where your inner silence is. Your inner silence is located within. You've always known this, but you have to reverse your eyes and reverse your ears to their original, primal position to actually obtain your central focus and realize where that eternal reservoir is to be found.

Now you know how to turn your internal dialogue off, and you know how your inner silence has identified itself in revealing its omnipresence, even though that quietude is intangible by nature.

Listen to what you can't hear. You can do it in every single circumstance. You can close your eyes and listen to what you can't hear. I'm continually applying this technique, twenty-four hours a day.

When I'm speaking, as I breathe, I don't listen to my breath, I observe what I can't hear within that. I'm watching my feelings, which are your feelings. I arrive upon you by arriving upon myself.

How can I know you if I don't know myself? The essence of how to know somebody else is to know yourself completely, by not having any feelings that are yours. This means to be located within that silent reservoir, which within itself is immovable, yet moved by everything.

This silent point of reference can be found within. From this central point everything can be felt and known, which means: I am myself, yet I am not. Or, you arrive but never appear.

When you don't have any feelings that are yours, the only thing you can arrive upon is whatever makes itself available. And as you happen upon somebody else within yourself while you're listening to what you can't hear, you find yourself speaking the dynamics of those feelings that have appeared within.

In reversing your eyes and reversing your ears, you now know how to listen to what you can't hear, look at what you can't see and feel what you can't touch.

INNER SILENCE

I want you to close your eyes and attempt to identify what you can't hear, by just breathing very gently and watching. As you locate this feeling, it expands. Your inner silence permeates not only the whole of your body, but extends beyond your limited confines.

Now my inner silence has arrived within your location and I'm with you. It doesn't matter that we are many thousands of miles apart. It's immediate.

Now open your eyes and be within this practice permanently.

In the end we are the sum total of our doings and we will be faced by those doings at the moment of our death.

Or is it our death in every moment that we live that faces us with what we do?

The Medicine Wheel of Wisdom

Amongst the emotional characteristics that have unfortunately been assimilated within human attention, the ones that require the strongest vigilance are the unwholesome projections that manifest as *poison dragons*, *white tigers* and *black widows*.

Each has a definite feeling in terms of the experiences obtained via the ramifications of their input. Those who harbor these maladies as usable tools to manipulate the world around them will find this chapter confronting.

The descriptions above are actually medicines, in the sense that the only way to cure yourself of a poison is to become aware of it. Corrupt tendencies need to be honestly viewed from within, until one cleanses oneself of these emotional imbalances.

The cure for energetic toxicity is the capacity to acknowledge what is festering within you via your inward gaze, thus neutralizing detrimental behavioral patterning through your pure introspective silence.

Once you understand the feeling that belongs to each, then the recognition of destructive traits becomes the wisdom of the beholder. A poison dragon is deceptive. A white tiger is violent. A black widow is treacherous.

It is now pertinent to warn you that the advent of your inner silence may give rise to unwelcome emotions. You will encounter the release of a great reservoir of distorted self-reflection by virtue of the fact that you have unplugged what has been hermetically sealed through your embedded, socially conditioned responses.

THE MEDICINE WHEEL OF WISDOM

They will reveal themselves to be untrue, and as this occurs you will be subject to them by virtue of the fact that your inner silence is exorcising those elements that are incompatible with its omnipresence.

By introducing the characteristics of medicine wheel I am going to describe how to cope and go beyond the negative sensations that may arise. At no stage are you to attempt ignoring these emotions. You must acknowledge them and embrace them for what they are.

As they present themselves they will identify their signature to you. As you realize that you have pierced a deeply embedded pustule it will be revealed for the stench and rot that it is.

When this experience comes upon you, do not feel guilty, nor remorseful, or use these items as the tools that once they were, cozily packed away within denial. Be patient and do not despair. You will soon understand what they are and how they will become wisdom for you.

As you witness this sickness arise you will become aware

that you were stricken. And as you purge I want you to watch these emotions and assign a name to them. The first one is the poison dragon; the second is the white tiger, and the third is the black widow.

When you look at these individually as something outside of yourself, you will know that the poison dragon is as such possessed with poison and can't be trusted. A white tiger is filled with rage and anger and deep resentments that wish to inflict its cruelty.

Then there is the black widow, who is treacherous and lurks deep within her secrets and shadows of deception, laying waste to everything, bringing ruin even to her own self to achieve that outcome.

These are outwardly viewed feelings for you now. Realize as they arise within that you recognize their traits, and know their actions can be neutralized through kindness and wisdom. Be empathetic towards yourself. Then these attributes become what you've seen and inadvertently what you know, in terms of how it came upon you and who applied whichever aspect you are aware of.

Know that they give you the medicine of sight, to reveal yourself as you arrive in the guise of those who approach. And as you absorb this folly you will know, beyond a shadow of a doubt, what you witness, and you will realize that it no longer belongs to you. For being within your silent service, a kind hand transforms the inhuman intent into the tangible, compassionate gaze within and without.

Now we will explore the practical techniques to overcome undue emotions and pressing feelings that may appear.

It's not what you believe that's important.

It's how you perceive what you believe.

Being, knowing, and doing

On to the teachings of *Being, Knowing, and Doing*, *Being, Knowing and Not-Doing* and *Knowing and Doing*. We'll give this subject a framework to help make the information readily applicable to all circumstances arising.

I'd like you to write down the word *Doing*. At the end of this word draw one line going upwards and another line going downwards. Now I would like you to write the words *Seeing* and *Liquid Confirmation* on the ascending line and on the descending line I would like you to write *Self-importance* and

Validation.

The true meaning of *being, knowing and doing, being, knowing and not-doing*, and *knowing and doing,* are very important principles to come to terms with.

As we discuss these concepts, realize that the descending line represents a plunging into the limited social eddy, whilst the ascending line represents overcoming that predetermined routine by doing what is unexpected, which is the *not-doing* of *being and knowing.*

What we're going to explore is what you can do with these distinctions. Know that most of the applied techniques governing the warrior's path are grounded in secret philosophies from the Orient.

The principles described have been referred to in some shamanic circles as controlled folly, but in reality there is nothing to be controlled and nothing, in actuality, is folly.

The concept of placing oneself in the position to judge

whether something is valid or invalid forgoes one's true ability to witness in absolute silence that which presents itself. Everything is there to be impartially observed as an essential element of our unfolding reality, that may later re-emerge to represent what was previously unseen.

What was initially introduced via these precepts was never fully accessible in the past, for the main teachers that disseminated this information themselves did not understand the real ramifications of these techniques as they weren't made available through the books they were reading.

The complete original teachings were kept as an indoor practice, in terms of gifting this knowledge to very devout acolytes only. As humanity has since broken through crucial thresholds within group consciousness I now believe that these teachings can be understood and applied in the manner intended, which is to conceive of the inconceivable.

In most cases, it's not what you do but what you don't do that delivers you to a state of personal power. This is the defining jewel that has been hidden from view and will be revealed in this text.

We're going to focus on these very subtle factors in terms of the intertwining elements that will form the impression-less impressions of the life that you lead, the road that you walk upon; your path with heart.

When you have your internal dialogue running on autopilot you forgo your silent truths. Your heart speaks the truth and knows the truth.

Remember that moment in your childhood when someone walked into the room, and they transmitted a feeling. You know exactly what you've experienced. You never talked about it, it just was. And as you read this sentence it just is what it is.

If you talk about a present circumstance in your adult life now, when you convey this information to another you are externalizing that experience through the mere act of verbal transmission, which is a self-important validation.

As you know, you've probably talked to yourself about it first; thus it has become scripted. When this script formulates, you move into a state of *Knowing and Doing*. Though the communication may seem to be self-empowering, it is far from it, for the lessons of your life path are trivialized by that exchange.

This gesture of *Knowing and Doing* can't be absorbed as one's true experience; it can only be applied as a false power or influence upon your environment.

This way of being is automatically connected to self-importance and validation by its very nature. The essential information becomes split and scripted and is traveled upon as a forked tongue, thus bypassing your inner silence into habituated narratives.

The essence of this forked-tongue can be simply described as saying one thing and doing another: "Do as I say but not as I do."

Though it is important to be aware of how this contradiction plays out in terms of action, it is not exactly what we are going to focus on here. What I wish to convey is how the forked-tongue principle has divorced us from our silence.

Knowing and Doing are complete within themselves in terms of providing a limited pre-programmed belief system that is applied as circular dogmas.

Though these doctrines appear to be all-encompassing, they are laden with a dominating principle of self-importance which creates the illusion of desire and need, whether that be manifest or indefinable; as in the case of the formulated idea of God.

This domineering perspective is also applied directly and indirectly to control underlings, or persons regarded as being 'incapable' of going beyond the confines of the limited ideologies that have been provided for what is deemed as their diminished state of consciousness; which has been purposefully cultivated in the first place.

All variants of this rudimentary control mechanism, which is an ongoing de-education, are based upon the same principle as the first lie that was given to you.

We believed in Santa Claus and as we grow we are told that there is a punishing god to secure our dependence via the idea that we need an external operative to govern our lives.

Remember this tactic that was used when you were a child: Be good and you'll get what you want, otherwise there is the threat of punishment. A prayer to obtain something is the same principle as focusing on a present under the tree.

That first constructive illusion now becomes the basis of a really dangerous false construct that can be endlessly manipulated to suit the distorted ends of that deception. This cloaked premise applies to all religions.

Realize that perceptual displacement is the basic

distilled program, which has far-reaching effects in terms of the internal ramifications set in motion. This premise can be utilized to secure the collusion of our awareness in being taken off point via the intricacies of polymorphic displacement in future circumstances.

This is the original sin; a Machiavellian sleight of hand that lays the groundwork for institutions hijacking our independence and is how organized religions, governments, and corporations gained so much influence and control.

The corrupt implications of that misdirection are a direct result of applying the very narrow parameters of *Knowing and Doing* in terms of how our eyes have been led away from their origin, their very being.

Everybody knows that the devil is in the details, and the complex minutiae are the elements that we are traversing the world with. They are the illusionary props of the limited knowings and doings that we apply; all of the social particulars that keep people comfortably embedded within the false freedoms and rights that each individual believes they have obtained.

The right to work yourself to the bone until the point where you have no energy left to even realize what you have been through, for just enough income to survive, appears to be the most subversive form of slavery that has ever been applied. This is just one example outlining the deceptive premise of a pre-programmed lifestyle and is a virtual summary of an urbanite's reality.

This type of awareness has nothing to do with our primal self and everything to do with our inner silence being re-diverted into channels that suit the requirements of a throwaway, mechanized society. Under such circumstances what we need to realize is our sovereignty, our capacity to be within our silence and to know what to do with it.

On your life path you traverse your experiences. There is nothing for you to really do other than that. You have to know how to proceed with these events.

Instead of a preformatted society prompting you into a state of *Knowing and Doing*, you need to return to a state of *Being, Knowing,* and the *Not-Doing* of yourself. And that *not-doing* is a partial experience of *doing* that automatically reverts back to *being*.

In any circumstance there are three steps to be taken. If one goes beyond these three, the fall is virtually irreversible. The fourth step represents a tactical illusion, where you attempt to find footing within the social moorings and you discover as you take that step that there's no ground to be found in terms of returning back to your essential being; that primal silence.

You are so stricken by this poison, this original sin, that intangible bite, that your descent becomes uncontrollable. The infliction of that blindness renders one truly mute to oneself, and the diverse elements of knowing and doing provide an endless and complex maze that obscures one's point of arrival.

That labyrinth always leads one away from one's

primordial matrix, providing the illusory calculus of knowing and doing that ensures that one never returns home.

This polymorphic process is continually constructing false conclusions that countermand the internal seer from discovering the true essence of their origins, where one knows the truth of what needs to be done in the moment that is continually escaping us all.

Ancient wisdom states that there are always three steps into the temple. The fourth is never there, for it represents a loss of one's true innocence.

These steps are inwardly traversed; by reversing one's eyes, reversing one's ears and anchoring one's inner silence by listening to what can't be heard.

The fourth step is represented by the internal dialogue, which is the trapdoor into *knowing and doing*. That device can be likened to the venom of the black widow, for it is a self-destructive and treacherous mechanism that is fully reflected in the times that we live in at this very moment, in the year early twenty-first century.

History will identify this period as characterized by self-destruction on many levels, not only internally reflected in our incapacity to see what needs to be done, but also externally manifesting as a physical reality of massive pollution and depletion of resources. This trajectory is a literal equivalency to poisoning ourselves and is leading to our ultimate demise if we don't change.

Know that this fundamental illusion was instilled before your original emptiness matured to the point where it could see itself from the perspective of a seer who has fully awakened to themselves.

What is vital to understand is that knowing and doing lead to self-importance and validation; and being, knowing and *slightly*-doing becomes the *not-doing* that immediately upon its internal realizations reverts back to its origins of being.

One's omnipresence *can* be regained, but when one is taken off point as a child, the original sin creates, in *knowing and doing,* a false ground to stand on, which in actuality is that fourth step taken.

We must clearly look into this reality as it is, and know that the *not-doing*s that manifest behind the veil of our conditioned expectations must first be applied in relation to what is readily available, in terms of all of the circumstances we have created for ourselves.

At the moment we are inescapably surrounded by our own species and the corresponding entrapments attached to that reality. Therefore the obvious workable elements are staring down the barrel of an etheric gun that is aiming its inevitability upon our life's journey.

Knowing this, one performs a miraculous declaration, and that is to stand fluidly and take responsibility for that oncoming enrichment as the *not-doing* of oneself.

Eternity is continually beckoning us away from knowing and doing, back to our true origin of being by giving resounding omens or indications that are invitations to return to our true nature. And this eternal omnipresence can be known, as an interdimensional anomaly that interacts with us so as to open our eyes to the only conclusions that we can come to, via its intervention.

Within this text techniques are given to identify those mysterious encounters so that, even though they will be experienced on this seemingly limited linear plane, the practitioner may realize what to do and what not to do with the influx of *not-doing*.

For example, the consequences of action in terms of self-importance must be clearly understood. When you listen to what you can't hear and look at what you can't see, and feel what you can't touch, you will be witnessing your arrival as a magical circumstance conveyed through that seeing.

If you communicate with somebody who is exaggerated

within their self-importance, you will see it and recognize it for what it is. By virtue of that display, you witness its folly. If you then speak to yourself internally in self-congratulatory tones for seeing another's validation or self-importance, you forgo your journey by interlocking that seeing with knowing and doing.

This then becomes your own original sin, inwardly reflected. Your self-importance automatically integrates with the same self-perpetuating loop that you are witnessing. This must be avoided at all costs.

Instead, when you view this validation, you know it immediately yet you don't need to talk to yourself about it, for you simply recognize what it is. Your inner silence gains gravity upon that threshold that has revealed itself to you.

When you listen to what you can't hear, your silence conveys that it is looking at what it can't touch; yet it feels what it knows, which in turn becomes a tangible item of seeing, thus revealing the center of your inner silence to itself.

While your awareness steps forward compassionately as a momentary doing, you inadvertently take two steps backwards within that inner silence that you discovered by listening to what you can't hear.

By virtue of this, your knowing sees itself and then immediately returns to its being, storing the event and changing the doing into a *not-doing* of one's sight, a *not-doing* of one's ears, and a virtual *not-doing* of one's self.

As an intuitive empath you know that when you listen to what you can't hear, you return to *being*. When you look inwardly at yourself with ninety-eight percent of your attention, you are discovering the feelings that cannot be touched yet are profoundly arrived upon.

As your gaze traverses its inwardly bound momentum, that carefully cultivated inner silence absorbs the event; not in terms of taking but in terms of that element observed becoming *being*: an item of power.

Realize that the absorption makes the item or event none of your business any more, which in actuality is the *not-doing* of *knowing and doing*, and this causes an omnipresent byproduct that will be further explained in later chapters.

When you know something, that information immediately transfers back to *being*. Your knowing of that circumstance is slightly a *doing*, which then becomes *being* instantly. As it travels back to its origin your inner silence opens up to itself within. It absorbs that experience as the power of the event you are witnessing.

 As this feeling becomes transformed within your silence you watch it and know it as the memory it was, simultaneously letting go of it. You don't talk about it to anybody, not even yourself.

You allow it to settle and be contained within your central matrix that is becoming the power that cannot be controlled. Within that silent reservoir it disappears. If it is let be, then this event that you have witnessed internally becomes interdimensionalized. It travels from you to somewhere else.

The only thing you have in your life is your own personal power. There is nothing else for you to bear witness to other than what presents itself to you. What you do with that is extremely important.

If what you are paying attention to is your own internal dialogue, you're listening to a repetitively adaptive script that bypasses the essence and unfolding subtleties of the moment that is continually escaping you.

Life can be a process of observing
what we are interfering with,
rather than interfering with
what we are observing.

The Art of Being, Knowing, and Not-Doing

Here we will further explore the art of being, knowing and *not-doing*. Throughout the entire text there will be repeated concepts to deeply contextualize the elements that need to be understood from multiple perspectives so that they can be fluidly applied in any circumstance.

Now remember, when you view your circumstances, if you see someone vaunting their point of view; know that in talking to you about it they are reinforcing a state of self-importance through this display of validation.

At this point you must realize that there are three steps towards your *not-doing* in terms of witnessing, or functioning within liquid confirmation via your seeing.

This state of consciousness does not speak to itself, nor does it speak to anybody else. It is a formless knowing that is transmitted through the fact that it is there and not there simultaneously, by virtue of how you perceive it.

When you witness the self-importance of another, be centered within your silent breath. As you listen to what you can't hear, you view what you can see externally and your body experiences it internally. You feel the encroaching elements that are the external operative attempting to gain momentum of over silence itself.

Do not struggle with it. See it by knowing it. As you know it, it is what you don't do with it that becomes very powerful.

Don't think about it. Be silent with it. Witness it. By doing this, your attention is applied as a *not-doing* of the social self, thus becoming a primal *not-doing*.

As this primal *not-doing* reveals the content of what you are witnessing within your body, you touch upon these feelings by watching them. They become information as you listen to what you can't hear.

What you can't touch then becomes a tangible item that is absorbed via the witnessing of that which is surrounded by your silence, your knowing.

This is how your knowing and doing becomes being. That event that becomes your liquidity is transported to your silent reservoir and is observed and thus absorbed, which is the only thing that can occur by virtue of the fact that this is what is happening upon your life path for you to encounter.

Now you are in a state of being and knowing. The acknowledgement of the partial doing that is your seeing is a tool to allow you to understand that your seeing can't be possessed. It is a metamorphosis that becomes the *not-doing* of yourself by virtue of disappearing within the central matrix of your inner silence.

This example shows the warrior that if the seeing is possessed it becomes knowing and doing, rather than knowing and *not-doing*. That silent absorption will happen if you don't talk to yourself about it. It happens because you don't justify your feelings. It happens because you let go of what you receive as soon as you witness it.

Everything becomes subject at this point to the doorway of your inner silence. The significance of what has occurred then becomes an item of power by not doing what you would usually do with it. The happening becomes the event that disappears from you at the moment you realize it, yet it leaves its indelible impression upon that part of you which knows what cannot be known.

This elusive moment is so intimately absorbed within the

center of one's power, yet upon its arrival becomes unrecognizable, even to itself. And these are the feelings that can be traversed and felt as your eyes inwardly track that which no longer has form.

Your eyes have decoded the onset of that emotion, which is a received doing from another, by transporting it back to the most essential part of yourself, your being.

This is where the warrior discovers the crucial distinction between feeling and emotion. Emotion is a frequency that can be looped within itself as a perpetual eddy that is ultimately defined by knowing and doing, and which relies upon an internal script.

In contrast, feeling recognizes itself momentarily as it's being seen. It has contours that illuminate its presence holographically. The feeling becomes a moment in time that recapitulates itself via your perception.

Even though it may originate from the external matrices

of another, it is a personal event to be observed from a seer's perspective as a glimpse of the moment that is continually escaping itself. This capitulation has no real parameters, nor dividing lines or divisions. It just is.

The parallel circumstance outlined in the previous chapter, in terms of the self-importance conveyed to you as a pure example of knowing and doing, can be understood as interfering with what you are observing.

There have been many well-documented studies by quantum physicists upon this phenomenon. They establish a field of observable matter and then arrive upon their circumstances expecting to understand that they can control the outcome of what they observe.

From a shamanistic perspective it is common knowledge that whenever the observer tries to interfere with the observable field their input automatically changes what they are witnessing.

For those scientists this posits a most difficult quandary. They see that what they observe individually changes in comparison to their observation, and when their colleagues come upon the same event, the observable field transforms anew in relation to the next observer.

Via their need to control what they are observing to obtain an empirical outcome, they are interfering with the very essence of that field, and this lays waste completely to the idea that anything can be definitively identified on the very subtle level of quantum matter.

This is the narrow field of knowing and doing. This premise perpetually loops in on itself as an eddy, for the observable field will never cooperate with the interfering observer. Thus any natural influx from this vibratory emptiness will not arise as an observable event that becomes insight so as to transform one's circumstance to the next plane of true realization.

Emptiness defines itself through the action of the

observer, which is why the appearance of the *not-doing* is so confusing for some. Understand that this is why a true prayer can never be prayed.

This conundrum is the quantum equivalent of the original sin, which is to be taken off point in terms of not accessing the essence of any moment in a correct manner due to habitual and preformatted expectations.

The second observable consequence of perception upon an event that is witnessed is the subtlest form of interference. That slight-doing is reverted into its *not-doing* by not investing ninety-eight percent of your eyes to that event. You only give it two percent, and though you've left an imperceptible mark upon that observable field, your soft glance is as light as a feather.

In so doing, the external operative that has been witnessed will realize that it is no longer being interfered with and will come upon the seer as a transcendental communication arising.

In other words, by *not-doing* the doing of that event, the field, which is eternity itself, then turns around and is automatically attracted by the emptiness presented, which allows it to recognize itself within you.

This is softly observing, through that *not-doing*. Whatever we engage, even if we see it and undo it by *not-doing* it, is touched upon by us, thus inadvertently altering that quantum field.

This is a general universal rule. To be in a state of *not-doing* is to gently observe what you are witnessing instead of overtly interfering with what you are observing.

Once you become aware of something, it changes in comparison to your observation. It is not what you do, it is what you don't do that delivers personal power to your inner silence… or your doings will inevitably undo that power in exchange for the social self.

Whatever you gaze at gazes back at you. Within this exchange you will always find yourself inwardly reflected. This is your heart of hearts, calling and responding to itself. When you listen to the song of a beautiful bird - when you truly listen - you hear yourself singing.

The bullet has only one gun

Bear in mind that there will be circumstances that will confront you that you may have to speak your truth to in the future, and this will require you to reveal your seeing, if that communication is pertinent and relevant to your path at the time. This voice is your true self-righteousness.

The most important thing to look at here is that there is a vital process inside of the body that protects our immune system. It is that state of self-righteousness. This is an instinctive alertness, an element that requires us to speak in a firm and direct tone and can be correctly applied to our circumstances, as long as it's done with power and clarity.

If you become aware of an item that is overly invasive from another, it won't be validation that comes to the surface to be spoken; it will be the seer arising from within to guard itself.

I do have to remind you though, that this subject is a very slippery slope in terms of utilizing your true voice in comparison to reinforcing a response based on validation or self-importance.

Let's just focus on the true self-righteous voice at this point. In the event of being put under fire via a circumstance that is inappropriate, your self-righteous voice can rise to the surface and speak the truth of what you've realized in terms of the assault you're under.

In so doing you are protecting your whole immunity, for

your happiness is as intimately linked to your well-being as your physicality. Remember, you can only speak the truth of what you see. You can't go anywhere other than the truth of what you know in that moment. And this is exactly the same as when you're on the battlefield.

When you feel you are under attack, your neuro-endocrine system becomes automatically active, thus in turn enlivening your immune system. Your voice can be used as a vehicle to neutralize negative onslaughts through its command, and is one of the chief protective mechanisms you have, which reveals your true feelings in comparison to the assault.

In a real life and death situation where an aggressor lifts his sword to lay waste to your life force, the only option that you have in this event is your reflex; a natural, inherent reactivity that saves your body from being wounded.

Our inner voice has the same function. But remember that when a truth is spoken it is like a gun that has one bullet.

The event can be spoken to only once, and the power of the aim and the trigger can only be applied to that circumstance *as it is, when it appears.*

If you are ever tempted to speak beyond the insight revealed to you, or justify your truth spoken, then you would expose yourself, not only to be attacked again from the outside but you would open up your own Trojan horse within, which begins to justify and reason its motives.

This in turn will bring back the most troublesome enemy that you have ever witnessed: The internal dialogue. Your self-justification and self-importance will attempt to regain the ground lost in terms of its battle with the inner silence that you have obtained.

The original thrust of your adversary will become aware of your internal reasoning in this instance and will attempt to inflame the inner calculus that you have so carefully extricated yourself from. Your assailant will sense this instinctively and begin to practice his reason upon yours. Thus the art of war will be applied to discover your strength and weaknesses in comparison to theirs.

One of the options in this situation is to speak with the strength of your integrity behind your voice, and thereby put a stop to the attack immediately. If you don't have the power to speak to that circumstance and you feel emotionally disrupted due to anger then you must acknowledge that that emotion is also connected to your own self-importance, and equally to your wish for validation.

Then being, knowing, and *not-doing* becomes knowing and doing, instead of seeing, and your need for self-assertion will engage that of your opponent, providing fuel for a repetitious enactment of that same battle of positioning, repeated in myriad manifestations of the tactics put forth.

Alternatively, another option when being assaulted is that you can retreat. In this circumstance, if you're in a state of liquid confirmation, which is your capacity to see and realize that you don't have the ability to speak to what you know, then you allow yourself to be aware and simultaneously wounded, which lays the fertile ground for your awareness to watch the feelings embedded within.

There's nothing else to be done in this situation, apart from bleeding. That bleeding also becomes your seeing, so you leave it in there as a vital point of reference to be witnessed, and you watch this feeling, which may arise to be spoken in a future circumstance; in an alternate event that could be totally unrelated to the previous experience.

In a state of being, knowing and *not-doing*, as you watch these particular feelings, you are then subject to what seems to be your emotion, but it's not really yours. It is actually an embedded feeling that is the attacker's assault, in terms of putting something inside your body, that is designed to harm you, which it will if you use it in a self-important manner, which is a knowing and doing.

You don't want to let that insertion fester into a destructive doing by adding your own self-validation to it. You need to leave it there and have the feeling sit within your body so you can watch it.

As you do this *not-doing*, you don't inflame it by giving it the same amount of energy that the person gave you, in terms of being totally emotional. You look at it impersonally by watching the feelings that arise from within.

While you view the internal event you allow it to generate energy that is contained within your being, but you never speak of the original doing that set this internal momentum in motion.

Allow it to convey the reflection of itself into your present moment as something new and eventful in terms of it becoming another insightful *not-doing* that witnesses itself through your experience of that complex interchangeable event that appears within a seemingly linear continuum.

Even though you may find yourself under undue pressure, your self-containment will yield wisdom and become a humble act of service. This is the *not-doing* of your *poor me*.

Otherwise said, it is the true application of your selflessness, for you did not reveal the self-perpetuation of the social script that is expected in terms of transference. In this way you ambush your socially-bound expectancy system, thus extinguishing your self-importance through this act of power.

Integrity in most cases is applied and rarely seen. The reflection of that is the only item that has real power — unspoken gestures or an action that may never be externally acknowledged bears relevance via its input or retraction from a circumstance.

These experiential items are only for you to witness, thus giving others the opportunity to really see you if they are fortunate enough to catch the event for themselves as an element of power that may be traversed.

One event becomes another through the act of service. You must remember via your experience to continue to relate to everybody in a kind and compassionate way in terms of being of service to their circumstance, for your downward gaze is inwardly bound.

Seeking Validation

In this chapter we will thoroughly examine the internal processes surrounding self-importance in order to further address this fixation that is so heavily embedded within our socially conditioned responses.

It is crucial to know what to do with not only your own self-importance but also that of others. Without understanding the full ramifications of this clandescent operative, our true magic will never unveil itself to be witnessed, individually or

SEEKING VALIDATION

collectively.

When you look at what you can't see, you watch the feelings that arise, and as this observation occurs you realize that you are transforming emotions into units of information that become items to be seen internally; even if they are externally located as a phenomenon being transferred via another human being.

As these components become fragmented or broken up into increments, you will begin to understand the process in terms of your inner voice speaking those itemized elements as the energy of your wisdom arising.

This internal anomaly is none of your business anymore, since you have let go of it, even though it is arising within. It is being witnessed — by listening to what you can't hear and viewing what you can't see — and is thus released from your grasp of understanding into your availability, which in actuality is your inaccessibility, even to yourself.

SEEKING VALIDATION

This inadvertently becomes your wisdom, how to speak the unknown, which in turn becomes your ability to be available to the world around you in terms of service. This magical process can be irretrievably fragmented through reverting back to your social script; your knowing and doing.

Personal power is gained through *not-doing* what is socially expected, so let's look at how this works.

It is essential not to talk to yourself about anything that you have realized, for once this occurs your internal dialogue will arise to congratulate you about what you know. As this pontification occurs between you and your Trojan horse you lose the essential essence of yourself.

Typically beyond this point you would share what you have seen, seeking yourself within the approval of another. As this occurs the nugget of wisdom is squandered as bait for a social self-gratification in terms of utilizing another human being's self-importance to validate those insights.

SEEKING VALIDATION

As you solicit their response toward your self-validating assertions you have lost your way, your heart of hearts, and you have also unwittingly drawn somebody else off their path through this process.

Even if that individual is already corrupted through their own behavior, any engagement of this nature further embeds the unwholesome imprinting that has established itself through their connections to the knowings and doings of their own life.

When you give over information to another, what they give you back is their opinion. Their point of view is almost invariably an idea formulated by or reflecting their own self-validation.

If you hand your experiences to someone else seeking validation, and they too are functioning from that basis, you can't trust the authenticity of the reflections they inject. Yet their input will become interwoven with your experience and will incrementally dilute and distort that information in the

SEEKING VALIDATION

bent of their realizations instead of yours.

That reflection has nothing to do with your seeing and their angle of perception may not really be in alignment with what you were realizing internally, which would have remained intact if it wasn't spoken.

By virtue of the fact that the exchange is based in the pseudo-transparency of social interaction, it's not going to give you true insight towards your life path, nor help the other person on theirs.

Even though you have recruited somebody to support and enhance your self-reflection, securing their alliance doesn't ensure that you'll arrive upon the essence of the insight that was hidden within that experience, waiting for you.

In actuality, you bypass the full scope of the realization that would have been revealed in time, had you relied on your own awareness to decode it.

Deep down you know that the resolve you seek will not

occur, for there is no way to genuinely align another person with a wounding that is meant to become your seeing. Transferring that wound to an external operative to procure advice will only trivialize and distort the true meaning inherent within it.

More often than not, an exchange of this nature caters to a needy desire to bond, to establish a connection via sharing personal information, which has to do with seeking to establish a sort of mutually protective agreement.

The other will find some way to enmesh with you in order to gain your alliance through their cooperative support of that self-reflection, which in actuality is validation seeking itself.

Let's say you travel on that emotion. You go home to your partner, who you love, and you know you have to deal with the seeing that's inside of you.

You want to speak to them because you need support, so

you may tell them about this, and perhaps the power of your seeing will be strong enough to organize what really needs to happen via the integrity transmitted within your communication.

But you nevertheless run the risk of falling into the closed loop of validation and not applying the real essence of that feeling to allow you to be compassionate towards your beloved, and to love and nurture them by not taking them off their path in sharing that information.

Validation is propelled by the internal dialogue, creating a chasm between you and the moment that is escaping you by perpetrating a false construct in terms of supplying momentum to justify a position; which further entitles the social self to reinforce or explain itself in a reasonable way so that it can continue doing what it's doing.

In other words, a person who validates through reasoning is simply doing what suits them and not what is actually relevant and necessary to be done, which is to follow their own life path and to reflect the cooperative elements of interaction; to resolve real circumstances and be purely within themselves by listening to what they can't hear instead of listening to what they've never heard.

When you are witness to a circumstance that impacts you, it is an opportunity for growth to occur. By transferring the personal relevancy of that data verbally to someone else you become blinded to the intricacies and value of that lesson that is so deeply bound to your path and is for your eyes and ears only.

You have to wait for the meaning to come to you. You can't take that experience and force it to be interpreted according to your wish to be recognized as the holder of the intangible that can't be held. Validation always seeks a mirror of itself, whereas seeing waits patiently for the unknown to appear.

As I am, so are others;

As others are, so am I.

Having thus identified self and others,

harm no one nor have them harmed.

Buddha

Bardo

At this very particular juncture one will begin to feel a loss, regarding the inability to communicate via the methods that one was familiar with previously. But in reality this is just the last vestige of self-importance clinging on, the way that is has always clung to you.

At this moment in your body there is truly an event horizon appearing. The loss at this stage cannot equal the gain. Watch deep within the feelings that appear, for if you observe *that which is,* becoming *that which isn't,* your sadness will turn to joy. Your feeling of your impending social isolation will transform to wonder and physical excitement.

We have spoken very clearly about what not to do in order to arrive upon the *not-doing*s of yourself. This last request is one of the strongest doings to be undone. Stop yourself in the midst of giving an opinion and wait for that insight to transform into the essence of itself.

As you undo your doing, knowing comes upon you as a wave of joy. By withholding yourself in restraining what was, you become willpower itself. Inside your body you will feel an enormous welling up of enthusiasm. You become joyous and released as if popping through into a new reality

As you survey the wonders that surround you, an eternal pressure will appear from within, providing the impetus to act without acting. Even if everything seems to be a mess, it is coherency itself in terms of how you are now able to see it.

Through your detachment you will act upon what needs to be done and your communication will emanate from itself enthusiastic and kind, loving gestures that are filled to the brim with the excitement of knowing that you have arrived.

When one leaves this mortal coil there is a point of levity, a place where one watches and sees what is, what was, and what will be. As this shift takes place, the imperceptible barrier that lies between the living and the dead is as it is: A veil that restricts the ability of the living to perceive the subtle realm where you have arrived.

You are there, yet you cannot speak. You are there, yet you cannot be felt. You are there, yet you cannot be seen. You are free at this point from what bound you.

As this occurs you begin to listen to what you can't hear, look at what you can't see and feel the vastness erupting from within. You become connected through that disconnection.

Eternity speaks through you at this transitional stage, and

if while you are living you reverse your eyes, reverse your ears and obtain the feelings you thought could not be felt, you arrive at your own point of transition by virtue of the fact that you are no longer listening to those thoughts, yet you are hearing what can't be heard.

You are looking at what you can't see and being overwhelmed by everything as it becomes you. You don't need to speak of it for it is already spoken. It is the original *word*. That inner journey is there to be experienced. This inconceivable transitional stage is almost always forgotten.

What I would suggest at this crucial juncture is that you wait patiently. Don't talk to yourself, nor to anybody else about the glimmers that you discover. They are for your eyes only.

When one is in a state of being, knowing and *not-doing*, insight arises as if from the edges of the inconceivable; in the contours of somebody's body, the vibration of a leaf on a tree, the stillness of a stone. Split the wood and you shall find yourself there.

You will always discover yourself inwardly reflected in terms of that exquisite encounter. Even though it's arrival is an external holographic phenomenon that nestles so closely yet is so far, it beckons and calls you to see it for what it is.

If you reveal that the leaf has moved for you and through that display has spoken to you of something that can't be seen, if the person to whom you describe this experience does not understand, they will say, that leaf is just a leaf, and as this occurs the precious insight or flower that appeared reverts back to the essential elements of itself. It becomes just a leaf. So be careful with your insights.

Unless your companions have the eyes to understand what you are revealing, it will not be seen. It will just be known as a social doing, that fourth step taken through the eyes of those who are not meant to see what you have delicately recognized.

This broken gesture will deliver you to no-man's land and leave you hovering in purgatory, an irretrievable place between the worlds of doing and *not-doing*, where you simultaneously witness and die to the mysteries of yourself by virtue of that premature communication.

You must dissolve your need to be reflected to allow that magic to reappear. This is one of the crucial *not-doing*s of yourself. Listening to what you can't hear, looking at what you can't touch, which in essence is inconceivably felt, you come upon the rarest sight that can ever be seen: A space, a point of reference in between realities.

This is the actual *not-doing* of your complete self. As you surrender, many things manifest to beckon you back. If you know the essence of the illusions that previously bound you, you will see them and know that they are not really there. Even though they have been witnessed, you must know that they are none of your business any more.

Once your original self becomes stronger than the scene,

or the life you lived, then your metamorphosis truly comes upon you.

Seeing is like a flower appearing, animated for a split second to be understood. It is recognized as a tangible influx that can be felt.

As you listen to what you can't hear, the fragrance of that epiphany wafts over you, and from within you realize what you know. It enters your bio-field and sits delicately within your inner silence.

As you watch it, the power from within you obtains that vision, that precious flower, by virtue of the fact that it has not been spoken.

As you absorb that communication through your ability to clearly see that formless form, it becomes a miraculous event leading to a point of enlightenment.

We are interdimensionally interdispersed entities. We are everywhere all at once. As human beings we are given a unique opportunity to understand this fractalization through witnessing it in the manner described.

As your inner silence absorbs this power, this insight, it automatically spins out of view. As this occurs each petal independently vibrates, returning as segments drawn to their origin-less origin, whose point of arrival is distinctly animated via the gravity of their purpose.

When your luminescence receives this holographic unit of information, it is simultaneously released and becomes vibration that attunes to its next destination. It comes upon itself elsewhere, and the seer awaits patiently for these fragments to reappear, applying the ineffable gesture of their inaction; the *not-doing* of that magical acquisition.

This is a pictorial explanation of silence and absorbing that pure epiphany that you never spoke to nor gave to anybody else. As this wordless integration occurs, power becomes recognizable to itself. It begins to look at what it can't see. It begins to feel what it can't touch.

It amasses within a place that can't be heard. It gains the magnetism of itself to draw upon that unknowable essence within the seer's act of *not-doing* what is expected.

These visual metaphors are well and good but there must be more explanation given. For that we will go back to quantum physics. Now remember when we spoke about that observable field, inadvertently becoming affected via the observer's impression.

No matter what we do, in terms of *not-doing*, we are moved, as is the field that we witness. The indefinable absorption that takes place is the recognition of that acquisition. There is a phenomenon called the observation of dark matter. Physicists are quite perplexed by this discovery.

In their attempts to observe the inconceivable they have learnt that at the basis of everything there is nothing to be found but the essential song or vibration that allows the viewer to stand at the edge of the abyss to find itself reflected in that which cannot be walked upon. Yet we do.

When they came upon this incomprehensible anomaly occurring, they assigned it the name *dark matter*, not realizing what they had stumbled upon. This phenomenon is much larger than the perceivable universe.

We are expanding exponentially from our source, yet the magnitude of that beginning is greater than what we could ever expect.

In the beginning, an infinitesimal expansion of light laid before itself a multidimensional carpet of endless realities. This has been referred to in the bible with the words, "My father's mansion has many rooms."

This description is a reflection of the realization that we are not only here, witnessing one singular reality on a linear plane. We are everywhere, inconceivably realized, and from that point the omnipresent darkness sees us, but we have forgotten how to recognize *it*.

It was noted by those physicists that dark matter does

not have a discernable pattern that can be identified and thus decoded. Where it comes from or where it goes to is completely inaccessible via a linear focus. It manifests as a random anomaly that has thus far only been identified via the expectation of what is to be seen.

In other words the observer has organized that arrival in a way that is recognizable to the reflective cognitive process of their perception, yet they don't realize the inherent beckoning of their own seeing.

In reality what they are witnessing is the entry point to the abyss, which has been reduced to an infinitesimal point of reflection by virtue of the fact that the perceiver can't cope with the immensity of that confrontation.

Our input invariably diminishes that awesome encounter to manageable, itemized elements that can be simply socially viewed, or primally seen. When the essence of this arrival is understood through consciousness decoding, this will mark the next leap of human evolution.

One of the significant developments pertaining to that event horizon will be the advent of the ability to transport the human entity from one time continuum to another. Teleportation will be realized as an interdimensional experience, not a linear timeline exploration.

This dark matter, this reoccurring random event, is a universal *not-doing*, an omnipresence isolated as a point of reference.

The seeing that comes upon a shaman as a vibratory moment to be witnessed appears with internally resonant data that is intimately interconnected to its point of origin that in essence is origin-less, multidimensional, and vast beyond measure.

This is the omen, the universal gesture, the *not-doing* of itself, to be witnessed as a seeing. It is the ubiquitous onset of knowledge from infinite perspectives to open the eyes of the beholder to view the vastness within.

It's not what you do.

It's how you do it.

Personal Power

Only the experiences of your life path, the struggles you have and the things you see, will deliver you to your personal power. If this is all you can obtain, then you had best be careful with what you do and what you don't do with what arrives in your body as pertinent issues to be witnessed upon your journey.

What you don't do really defines what you end up doing as a human being. It may be that less is more.

When you witness your own omnipresence, which you arrive upon through listening to what you can't hear, seeing what you can't view, and touching what you can't feel, your inner silence opens one of the essential gateless gates for your power to enter.

When it comes upon you, you must not assume that you will automatically or immediately access the full spectrum of information contained within that experience, simply by virtue of the fact that is has gone through your gateless gate.

Receiving insight is like being subject to light filaments that contain data. As we spiral through the universe, if we listen to what we can't hear, looking at what can't be seen and obtaining what can't be felt, this first formless threshold allows one's perception to absorb on its journey the portion of light that it is passing through.

Similarly, the earth is mirroring us, in that it travels through the universe obtaining information, absorbing the light from each quadrant it traverses, for it too is primally bound to its own essential nature, which is also ours.

We are subject to the information contained within these delicate filaments that are journeying through and beyond the quadrant of the universe that we are advancing upon, in cooperative symbiosis with our planet.

The earth sings, as we do, the frequencies that reflect its essential nature, and these are true gestures. It does not presume nor assume to judge or be judged upon its arrival and departure. It just is as it is. So to reflect this very simple wisdom is to be as our earth is: A living conduit.

We are akin, by virtue of resonating within analogous bandwidths, of which there are thousands emanating from their source. Unfortunately at the moment we are incrementally breaking down these subtle emanations, drastically reducing the structural integrity of the frequential spectrum through the destruction of our natural environment.

In the present industrial age the essential nature of

ourselves and the planet are rapidly plummeting into a state of no return. If we do not realize that our present knowings and doings are gravely discordant with our combined destinies, we will bring about our own demise.

This catastrophic state of affairs can be reversed if we return to our primal nature and begin to realize that we are symbiotically bound to our natural environment; through listening to what we can't hear, which in essence are those thousands of frequencies holding our bio-field intact through our combined power of connectivity.

Whenever any information is obtained by our inner silence it becomes dispersed within our personal power, and the process of the absorption of those frequencies is automatically out of our grasp. If you see it, you know it and then you must wait for it to blossom within, so that you can completely realize it.

If you don't talk to yourself about it, the first gate opens up to absorb what you know, to become your internal seeing by virtue of that containment; which turns the whole personal experience into an impersonal affair, since it is none of your business to interfere with that encounter.

This allows it to be free of you and you free of it. Thus the essential destination of that abstract acquisition will be determined via its inherent gravity, and not your decision to obtain a reasonable outcome that can only suit a self-reflective loop that is humanity's Trojan horse, the internal dialogue.

Remember, if the unrelenting nagging of your inner knowing and doing does not attempt to possess this seeing it will be reorganized via the resonance of its own density, in terms of its immersion within the power contained that you no longer have any control over, for you have let go of it.

Thus this phenomenon harmonizes itself with the quadrants of the universe that you are ineluctably traveling through by virtue of being a passenger upon this blue planet.

The way that this works is that you have phase elements

continually going in and out of your body, through what in Lo Ban Pai* we call Shen Gongs.

A Shen Gong is an interdimensional porthole, that appears etherically to be shaped like a spiraling cone, mimicking the very nature of our reality energetically. It is a true reflection of the golden equation or the Phi ratio.

This echoes the way that our planet coils through the universe. It is the same phenomenon you will see in a tornado, or when water empties from a sink; a spiraling form that is a reflection of this invisible mathematical equation that appears everywhere. Even the pores of our skin, seen microscopically, appear as if looking down into a hurricane from above.

All movements that follow this coiling principle create these magnetic openings, and when you listen to what you can't hear and view what you can't see, you are in actuality

---

* *Lo Ban Pai* is a complete system of movement taught by Lujan Matus. For detailed information please visit his website.

waiting for one of these points of arrival to appear.

If you look at a living organism, whether it be a plant, an insect or an animal, this equation, this golden ratio, is available by virtue of it being lived through that physical creation.

In shamanism it is not the jaguar or the crow that has meaning, it is what follows from whatever you view as an energetic transfer. This element travels upon these light filaments and delivers a momentary jolt or glitch within one's matrices. At this instant of consonance the seer downloads pertinent data that is necessary for their evolutionary process, assisting them to realize their very purpose for being.

Thus that fleeting exchange is the moment delivered to the inner silence of the one who waits patiently for it to appear, even though there is no patience applied. One must wait without being aware that they are waiting.

Via this simple fact, a seer cannot presume to determine what will be delivered to their life path, nor seek with intention what they desire to find. In reality you can't go out into the woods and shake a rattle around a campfire, whispering "intent" and expect returns from this activity.

Personal power defines itself through re-emerging appropriately upon a circumstance that is relevant to a person's life path, which equals their vibrancy in terms of the bioelectrical vibrations they are emanating.

As this precious influx is absorbed through one's silence into the basis of one's personal power, it becomes equivalent to what is known as a phase particle. Disappearing to itself, it aligns with its destiny by obtaining the necessary frequency to open the gateless gate of the time-space continuum where it will next arrive upon itself, and thus be received in accordance to the magnetic necessity of that circumstance.

Harmonization is the vital equation, the key to obtain entry to its new destination, whether that point of arrival be past, present or interdimensionally located.

This magical occurrence is most often experienced when one is engaged in the act of being of service to one's circumstance, whether that be a human interaction, or something as subtle as being directed harmoniously through the frequency obtained within your body, such as when walking through a rainforest. You always are where you are meant to be.

Once you realize what you need to do, you simply stop doing what you were doing and apply yourself to what must be done. Where we are stuck as a humanity is in persistently doing what we want to do, in comparison to what we need to do.

The simple answer to this quandary is to accept and take responsibility, thus neutralizing one's self-importance through withdrawing that mood and becoming of service to that which cannot be controlled. Personal power is an impersonal affair that can only be applied, not acquired.

Never forgetting is not really remembering.

Advanced Recapitulation

Recapitulation is absorbing the vital moment to summarize what are the most essential points that come to the surface to be noticed. Compared to the living essence of what is being directly experienced, anything else is superfluous.

This is a very complex subject, one that is not easily comprehensible, which we will now look at from different perspectives to help bring about a deeper understanding.

When one uses the social self to decide the direction of

recapitulation, that focus will direct one's reviewal in terms of validating the knowings and doings of a pre-existing mindset.

Realize that this is not recapitulation. It is soliciting an outcome that suits self-reflective contours that support and protect one's self-importance with layers of social complexity that may have nothing to do with what needs to be undone.

On the other end of the spectrum, the primal self will wait for the essential to arise, in terms of receiving the essence of what appears in one's present moment continuum.

Embodying recapitulation as a practical application to one's path means not living the way you used to live, and being so completely in the moment that you are lost to yourself. This awareness is attained by completely being of service and witness that to which is continually escaping you.

To truly review in this state is to subtly observe what appears within your biosphere from the indications received, forgoing the need for validation, which in essence is social recognition.

You are renewed via the fact that you are not continually reinforcing your program, and thus are receiving the unknown through this emptiness, which is the true reflection of the ever-present pressure that supplies the impetus for you to see it. This is to be in a state of being, knowing and *not-doing*.

When interacting with another you learn to speak the knowing of the interweaving tapestry that has arrived in your body as feeling. Your eyes become a vehicle of communion, not of scrutiny. You apply this connectivity to be of service to others on behalf of the pressure that is present in your biosphere.

This is one of the arising dynamics that will reveal itself to you via your personal power. As a conduit of service, you know that any item that is deposited as a feeling is there to be reviewed by virtue of the fact that it has come upon you. The circumstance conveys itself through the inward reflection that is the receptivity of your body consciousness to internally mirror itself to you as a feeling.

When we listen to what we cannot hear we arrive upon our sacred self; a silent reservoir that recognizes what is being felt. As you cast down your eyes, what appears is an external holographic image that cannot be seen via a social perception but is acknowledged by an intuitive empath as a memory that can be felt in the moment that is continually revealing itself upon its departure.

Here the eyes focus upon a point of no arrival that can never be obtained, yet you are delivered. When this occurs, you breathe in very quietly and review the internal realizations, which are the present feelings made available, through listening to what cannot be heard.

Once this manifests, the next crucial step is to speak of the unspoken. This literally means that the gravity arrived upon, or the energy of one's own internal realizations in terms of that recapitulation, becomes available as a vehicle of communication for the collective advancement of the circumstance.

You speak to what is relevant for others, not on behalf of the relevancy of yourself, thus what is personally realized is impersonally applied. This creates a unique state of isolation which becomes an all-encompassing union by virtue of the fact that one's own self-importance is completely neutralized, giving light to the genuine need of the given circumstance as a focal point of devotion.

Through this selfless application you will be inadvertently faced with yourself, if you are internally there to be found, and inevitably your gestures will have a domino effect, reaching far beyond the immediate sphere of enactment.

The seer gains enormous distance from their present circumstance as a result of their non-enforcement of their own needs. They remain outside of that social sphere, yet intimately connected to every facet of what comes upon them and absolutely dedicated to that which presents itself at every single moment.

In biblical terms this technique has been illustrated via the saying, "Be gentle as a lamb, yet wise as a serpent."

To be gentle is to be innocent. To be young and vibrant as a lamb is to be buoyantly and lovingly involved and thus vulnerable. To be as wise as a serpent indicates that your eyes have great acuity recognizing all complexity within the simplest act.

This attention represents wisdom, absorbing the underlying truths portrayed in any living circumstance within its unrelenting gaze. The serpentile aspect is only a grain of sand in comparison to the depth of the ocean that can be portrayed via the open-heartedness of the lamb, yet they complement each other perfectly via their living equilibrium.

Whilst the serpent's acuity gives a necessary gravity, it is only through vulnerability that one gains access to the interdimensional subtleties of one's circumstance. Within this complex metaphor, one cannot survive without the other.

Be within the moment where you innocently act, yet observe what is meant to be seen as it arises, patiently waiting, without expectation, for the circumstance to unravel and evolve as it is, without a word spoken, not even to oneself.

This method of recapitulation uses the impetus of feeling to be brought to the surface as an ultimate tool for self-realization. You speak to that arrival yet never reveal directly those aspects that are for your eyes only, which will become increasingly apparent to you as you progress upon your path.

By observing and giving voice to the essential portions of that complex tapestry that you must, your input will become a true gesture of devotion and power.

This is recapitulation from the perspective of a seer. It is a totally different affair to employing a step-by-step approach to dissolving one's personal history via methodical emotional analysis.

ADVANCED RECAPITULATION

Always remember that feeling is what arises and emotion is something that we add, which is a call for validation. Feelings are symbiotic with seeing; emotions are requisites of self-importance. If you operate with your feelings in the way that we've discussed, they become an indispensible compass upon your life path.

Be careful not to function from the basis of emotions, for your fixation will take you and others on terrible detours off their life path, since you're traveling upon something that is neither relevant nor real.

When confronted by an experience that challenges you, you essentially have two possible responses. The first is feeling offended or sorry for yourself and seeking validation. The second is to be humble to what's happening, since any situation opens a door for true communication to take place.

The moment has given you the impetus to see beyond the petty incident that occurred. Instead of drama, that event brings wisdom. It's very beautiful.

ADVANCED RECAPITULATION

If you use any circumstance as a vehicle of validation, you follow a road that entraps and imprisons you. If you go the way of service and not seeking recognition, you embark on a magical path, upon which you have no idea where you're going to end up.

You phase in and you phase out, just like dark matter. That is letting power itemize you instead of you itemizing the elements of your world.

You listen to it, and you know you can't hear it. You watch it, and you know you can't see it. You feel it, and you know you can't touch it, yet what arises is such a strong reality within. As you apply this delicate observation your seeing is relayed to your inner silence.

The moment is absorbed interdimensionally into other aspects of your being and then delivered back to you as true information; as insight, as excitability, as a point of union, where you can only be grateful for the mystery of what has graced your path.

ADVANCED RECAPITULATION

This entire book is wholly focused on the practical application of advanced recapitulation from an intuitive empath's perspective. The essence of this refined attention can be arrived upon through using one's inward gaze so as to allow oneself to be transported, linearly and interdimensionally, within and beyond the confines of all living constructs.

When you listen to what you can't hear, viewing what you can't see, ninety-eight percent inwardly bound and with two percent of your attention softly connected to that cursory glance, this triggers the outward gaze to expand, seemingly via its own volition, and simultaneously the fibers that are enlivened via the seer's concentrated attention become exponentially activated.

From within the empath's luminous viscosity the internal essence of their perception expands in comparison with what is being gazed upon. This can be likened to energy emanating from an extremely hot marble ball.

The density of the source remains constant within its

gravity while the emanating heatwaves, which are a representation of the seer's two percent cursory glance, expand outwardly.

Those emanations nevertheless remain permanently connected to the magnetic source that is the empty attention of the empathic view, for the hand would never divorce its own heart.

To further illuminate this subject, we will return to reexamine the extremely subtle, rarified plane of existence known as bardo. Imagine within your mind's eye the smoky filaments of luminosity that reside there, awaiting to be retrieved, even though they can't be visually apprehended.

When one listens to what can't be heard one obtains what can't be seen or felt by a socially orientated being. As the seer gazes within, witnessing the omnipresent silence, these tenuous threads that are connected to the luminous field draw upon the unknown essence of bardo and are absorbed by the *not-doing* of the inner being of the shaman.

ADVANCED RECAPITULATION

There are memories stored in bardo that can be absorbed via the intuitive empath's attention in terms of recapitulation within the act of gazing.

For example, when the seer places their attention upon the flames of a fire, ninety-eight percent of their gaze is automatically inwardly bound, thus setting forth the external emanation of that two percent by-product.

Information will be forthcoming in comparison to the energetic matrices of that porthole which is the item being gazed upon. The two percent of attention focused outwardly gains access to the elemental structure of the information that is stored in the Akashic* file accessed via that act.

When gazing at fire, mountains, pools of water, stars, or any such object, one obtains the vibratory essence of that which is seen, intermingled with information that pertains to

---

* The Akashic files are universal blueprints where all information resides.

the object gazed upon, within its own fractalized dispersion, interdimensionally, which could inadvertently include the memories of a Tibetan lama or an ancient shaman that lived in the Altai regions thousands of years before.

One must take into account that each object gazed upon has a particular frequency that affects the personality of the seer. If focused on obsessively, this can distort the intention of the gazer toward that mood, in some cases irreversibly, especially if what is accessed is incompatible with human attention.

So remember to empty yourself of what you have obtained by continually listening to what you cannot hear, thus arriving upon the emptiness that is within form; and this is the true reflection of what has been gazed upon.

Through the power of gazing one can even go so far as to discover a future incarnation without entering bardo, thereby assuring that the resonant frequency of that consciousness is successfully transferred via the gazer's empty intention.

Even though the shaman in the past and the shaman in the future are both living in separate time continuums simultaneously, the shaman who has the most power can make a conscious leap to his future or to his past via the interconnective ability to access the Akashic records that pertain to their traversing.

For example, if a shaman fire-gazes and then is transported through those flames to his future self, portions of his memory will be kindled within that lifetime, as long as that future being is open to receive the subtle frequencies transported through that gazing.

This has occurred with me. I have seen my future in 2512 and this experience allowed that continuum to return to me, thus influencing my direct *not-doing*s as valuable input to support the future and the past ramifications of my two lifetimes. In essence this means that the future has affected my past and the past is affecting my future.

Even though bardo is empty of itself, the future and the

present that are being limboed in-between, which are concretely recorded within the Akashic records, are intimately connected with that realm. However, what has been stated does not indicate linear continuity in terms of outcomes.

In other words, destiny is not pre-determined along the narrow precepts of knowing and doing in terms of obtaining what you expect, for we are interdimensionally interconnected and each element acted upon assigns an alternate future to manifest. There is nothing linear about it.

You can always expect the unexpected. You never get what you want, you always get what you need; and this is fractally determined within such a complex mirrored matrix that if you would visually see it occurring you would literally soil yourself.

Now let's look at the life of a Tibetan Lama to draw a parallel in terms of assimilating this complex continuity. When the Lama is born, he is discovered as a child and then instructed on how to obtain Buddhahood through the study of innumerable texts and correct action, via the example of the monks that tutor him, thereby allowing him to gain the gravity of his previous memories in this lifetime as a result of that concentrated effort.

Remember that if the Lama was not discovered then he would live his life as a normal man, thus forgetting who he was, leaving all previous lifetimes within a virtual limbo.

If the very same lama is discovered five hundred years in the future, the previous information that a fire gazer may have obtained in the meantime will still be accessible to that Tibetan in the future, unencumbered in any way, regardless of whether another shaman had accessed their insights through the act of gazing.

In other words, they are available and intact within their resonant frequency, which means that the possibility for that information to be obtained and re-disseminated will always be there, in the Akashic files.

If a shaman is reborn and does not recommence his journey, thus retrieving the information previously accessed, the filaments, the light fibers, will disconnect, due to the fact that the two percent of his attention has failed to reach out to his full potential to retrieve his past memories.

Thus he will wander lost to himself within the social knowings and doings that will encompass him within his present lifetime, instead of the *not-doing* of who he was and can become.

To listen to the unspoken

is to hear what can't be heard.

Listening Power

We've taken one step forward, now let's take two steps back. Even as you arrive upon the most powerful *not-doing* there is, the unknowable, you are nevertheless confronted by the ever-present pressure of that which encircles you: Humanity. We are surrounded.

Everybody is affected by the fact that we're constantly immersed in the atmosphere of all the people that are around us. The only way to get to the deeper experiences that will lead to real progression under such conditions is to actually talk about the circumstances that impact you.

Even though this may seem contradictory in terms of everything else that has been taught within the principles outlined, there is a very good reason for engaging in sincere and heartfelt verbal communication. It is to allow that experience to unfold within you, via waiting for what is to be voiced, which is the *not-doing* of spoken interaction.

Although the particular narrative example of Father Christmas and the first lie is a narrow vehicle of discovery within itself, almost everybody on the planet has had the experience of being given that first lie; the first manipulation, or the first instance of becoming validated through self-justifying the need to want more than what is really necessary for your life path.

We must recognize that we cannot escape the consequences of the momentum that has beset us within our consumer mindset. Knowing this, one is required to incrementally change one's attention in comparison to that ingrained mechanism.

By becoming intelligently aware of the impact of our own actions through our immediate environment we are able to slowly discern what is positive and negative, as opposed to blindly accepting what we have been programmed to believe is right.

If when you learn about these things you experience difficulty coming to terms with the unfolding negativity of the world's present paradigm, sharing experiences can build a bridge of discernment.

For even though you can't really equate the absolute complexity of world circumstances to your personal experience, they are intimately connected via the fact that in both realms there are many veils that misdirect us away from the essential elements that must be applied for our progression, as individuals and as a species.

To further understand this veiling principle, one simply can observe one's own process of denial, which is a direct reflection of the ever-present imbalances that are affecting us all.

The very process of listening to what you can't hear and looking at what you can't see allows one to become acquainted with the intangible, which we are immersed within yet subtly removed from via the social eddy that binds us to the internal dialogue instead of the power of recognition that is naturally inherent within us.

What we have become accustomed to witnessing is a social illusion that takes precedence due to the fact that the process is so intrusive that it becomes difficult to bear witness to the unobtrusive, which is so subtle in comparison.

Have you ever been in a picture theatre and you momentarily look at the back of someone's head and they turn around to meet your eyes, as if answering your call?

LISTENING POWER

We have all experienced being watched and physically responding without knowing why, to be greeted by the eyes that were inquiring after our attention.

This one simple example is the most recognizable occurrence yet the hardest to fathom, because of the mere fact that what we knew wasn't consciously acknowledged, yet our body responded to the call.

These are the subtle factors, the nuances that are our true self, our primal being communing on a level of consciousness that must be brought to bear witness, so that we may reclaim what has been lost through our conditioning. We must truly believe that these possibilities are tangibly available, in every single moment.

When one refuses to listen to their own self-validation and the incessant nagging of others' need to be validated, the most powerful gateless gate opens, inwardly toward our inner silence, to present to us that we have a choice, yet no control over the outcome.

Thus we become subject to the manifestation of that which was previously unrecognizable via the fact that the veil of our self-importance had guided us away from the essential truths of our reality.

As a child or a empath, we assimilate information through the capacity of our body to feel. This ability is the external application of the *not-doing*s of the first gate, which is seeing by listening to the call of your feelings. It is an unrung bell that is ever-presently heard.

This state of being is the activation of primal attention that was absolutely necessary in the not too distant past to protect one's very being; in battle, or in circumstances such as traveling between villages or provinces, or sleeping in the wilderness and having to defend oneself or to be one step ahead of impending circumstances. A primal being functions with a heightened sensitivity, regardless of culture.

It is essential for us all to focus on what can't be known, so that it will manifest itself in comparison to the seer who makes themselves available to it.

When a *not-doing* comes upon you, and there is no reflection of yourself to be found, many things can and will be related back to you as knowledge, yet you have no way of knowing how you assimilated that wisdom.

Via reversing your eyes, reversing your ears, and listening to what you can't hear, you access the first gateless gate. It's a very complex portal to come to terms with in the beginning, since all of the techniques to access it are *not-doing*s of the social expectancy system.

You learn to perceive what you can't see, you learn to sense what you can't touch, and you are listening to what you can't hear. You are in a primal state of awareness.

This *not-doing* needs all of these elements to be put together, in terms of your eyes being inwardly bound, ninety-eight percent, and the ears externally bound, one hundred percent, so that you can begin to listen to the world completely and watch yourself absolutely. Yet all the while your two percent cursory glance touches the world very lightly, like a feather.

You never leave yourself as an impression upon the world. The world always leaves its impression upon your silence. This is how we travel as seers, upon this feather-light touch.

Your listening power is the application of being, knowing, and the art of *not-doing*. Your being, knowing and *not-doing* is active and relays a message to you which has nothing to do with you, yet alerts your body of the oncoming information that is heading straight for you.

The way one develops their listening power is basically by watching what can't be heard. This is *not* paying extra attention to the details of that which is auditorily available, but truly listening to what one cannot perceive.

The complete *not-doing* is to look at what you're

listening to, be aware of what you're feeling when you do this, and watch with your interdimensional capacity to peruse your present circumstances. Even though we are contained within linear continuity, this is far from being the whole picture.

We are interdimensionally active within this construct. We are constantly receiving messages via the frequencies sent and obtained by the antenna of our biosphere.

Our journey in this plane is a practice ground to become intimately connected to the fragments of awareness that arrive from alternate constructs, which are located within their own linear timelines and enter ours as compartmentalized items to be assimilated within our present time continuum.

In other words, we can receive a message from our self two hundred years previously, as an active memory that appears within a moment; an epiphany that enhances the present continuum as a futuristic aspect of the past.

When you become aware that you are continually

practicing these *not-doing*s, all aspects of one's self meld together as a primal attention.

Our listening capacity is enhanced by activating one's luminous fibers, which naturally infinitely extend in and throughout all living constructs and time continuums as innumerable threads that are incalculably assigned as the fundamental basis of *all* realities.

Like pulsating signals that resemble our neural network, one lifetime or one time continuum is a receptor that will receive the pertinent amount of information in comparison to what is needed within the scope of that reality.

To further expand upon this subject, the luminous, rope-like threads that extend from our biosphere can be tangibly felt as conduits of impulse that seem to be whipping outwardly and inwardly simultaneously, yet are so subtly received that they are almost invisible to us. They momentarily oscillate upon their receptor site and are interpreted via our chakra system.

Upon the arrival of that feeling we know what we have received, yet have difficulty detecting the origin until we master our capacity to be within our own deep resonance of inner silence. This is a lifelong journey that encompasses everyone we have ever been.

One way to experience the tangible sense of what has just been described is to climb a mountain with high vertical cliffs or crevasses. Sit very close to the edge, tie a rope around your waist to secure yourself, and sleep there for the night, or a whole week if you like. Position yourself maybe two feet away from the edge.

The cliff has to have a fairly steep drop to create some sort of feeling of vertigo, or the sensation that you're going to fall. What you will experience is the pull of these fibers extending themselves.

When your body falls asleep, before it does so it searches the environment as an act of present recapitulation, to discover the contours of its containment.

With this technique the palms and soles of the feet are activated, and the impression of plummeting is deeply recognizable within one's biosphere.

One does not use these ropes purposefully. They act of their own accord. You can achieve the very same result by tying yourself to a very high limb of a tree and staying there for the night.

On a cliff top, even though you are at a great height, your feet are still on the ground. Similarly, in a tree you are grounded by virtue of its roots being embedded in the earth.

In a modern building, however, it is quite common that the electrical grid that is installed isolates us from the electromagnetic field of the earth, so it is best to go into the wilderness to experience this.

These techniques will enhance the first gate — which is comprised of reversing your eyes, reversing your ears and listening to what you can't hear — by giving a real, tangible feeling of the ropes.

This can be interesting if one feels it is useful to physically connect to the sensations that are developing, but it is not absolutely necessary to go out of one's way, for these feelings will develop on their own without pushing one's body to its limit.

When the filaments extend like this in your environment, you are exercising the same faculty that you use internally to listen to what you can't hear, look at what you can't see and feel what you can't touch.

These active conduits host the ninety-eight percent of your attention that is focused within, thus enhancing the two percent extension of the feather-like perception that is universally connected. They interphase with, and are located by, the enormity of the *not-doing* they encounter, which fills the seer with knowledge or acts upon their circumstances as magical occurrences that are connected to interdimensional gestures of an omnipresent being that cannot be completely known.

When you sleep or are in an awakened meditative state these fibers become very strongly nestled within one's biosphere, whilst simultaneously activated externally. They interpret the deposited information that becomes intense feelings upon contact with one's circumstances, whether manifest within linear or interdimensional interaction.

These super-conductive threads are ultimately subject to the most powerful *not-doing* that exists, an ubiquitous darkness or void-like substance that is aware of itself and extends beyond anything we could ever imagine.

I must clarify at this point that if the fibers are overly focused on (in terms of the cultivation of *Ting Jing* to become *Fa Jing*[*]) then you risk forgoing the greater subtleties of the journey that you have embarked upon, and the absorption of

---

[*] See Glossary

the realizations of how your circumstances shift harmoniously in the absence of your willful intervention.

If a gesture is the most powerful command that you have,

then words mean very little.

Gestures of Spirit

*Not-doing*s of an enigmatic yet immediate nature are the way that eternity communicates with us. It interacts through indications, for it does not utilize language as a medium.

Words actually mean nothing in comparison to the experience that we are having, and however you are introduced to your destiny through these moments, no one can predict or determine the outcomes that will bear relevance to your personal journey.

It is only your experiences that count, in terms of your perception locating the identifiable points of meaning for you. The further you traverse upon your path the more adept you become at assimilating these omnipresent communications.

Almost every single instance reveals an omen. It's a communion that goes beyond any semantic exchange, or any kind of emotional transfer, for it is the true essence of the circumstance that makes itself available to you.

The unknown cannot present anything other than *not-doing*s, and it is continually observing our awakening toward these events.

The only way to recognize the knock of Spirit is to truly be empty and in a state of receptivity. You have to be listening to what you can't hear at all times.

You can't have an internal dialogue. You can't be socially bound. You must indifferently watch your circumstances yet be lovingly involved. You have to be in a state of *not-doing* yourself.

Then something will begin, inside of you and outside of you, to allow you to be aware of the omnipresent silence that is forever witnessing you, and to give you certain confirmations that you are still on track, even though you may not know exactly how to proceed upon your journey.

Gestures of Spirit are those indications from the unknown that beckon our attention beyond the explicit by sending signals to show us that we are actually on our path with heart. The confirmation of this omnipresence is always felt.

You have to be open to the communication, neither losing it within social moorings nor rushing to interpret it so as to procure an outcome. That mystery must be left to flow like an endless river that will carry you upon your destiny.

Although there is no way to wield intellectual certainty as a means to appropriate an act of power, once that omen appears it becomes fluidly recognizable via the fact that your silence absorbs it at its point of arrival.

Your body will compel you to proceed in a way that is harmoniously and progressively moving toward the gravity of your personal power. The indications that arise, within and without, always propel you into the next phase of your life and make you stronger and more aware, yet in a way that reduces your idea of yourself.

To give one concrete example of what *may* occur, and did occur in my life, in terms of multidimensional interchanges that arise during moments of synchronicity, I have included this account of an event that took place during a training session in Thailand.

I asked my student, Margel, to relate her experience of this magical occurrence that highlights possibilities far beyond what we have been taught to expect.

I was instructing her in the art of *Lo Ban Pai* and while

we were training the form known as Dragon's Tears, the following anomaly made itself available to both of us.

We completed the whole form of Dragon's Tears *ahead of time and on this particular day, Lujan was teaching some final refinements of the gestures I was learning.*

Facing one another, we performed the elegant spiraling movements of Dragon's Tears, *completely absorbed in a state of profound inner silence.*

I was observing my body fluidly mirroring Lujan when I had a flash of insight that took me by surprise. It was a bodily sensation and at the same time, a feeling of déjà vu. It struck me that I had done this before with him, and yet, in this lifetime, I had not met Lujan until now.

As soon as this perception came upon me, Lujan immediately spoke, "You young whippersnappers! Here I am teaching you once again," he said, laughing at my astonishment.

Though I didn't say a word about what I had seen, he further confirmed what I was realizing by stating that he had had a vision of us in Tibet, performing the movements in a room full of flickering candles, hundreds of years ago.

When we finished the Dragon's Tears *he discussed with me how the memory came to him upon the moment of my déjà vu. He had seen a complete picture within the mirror hanging on the wall behind me and to the left.*

He then proceeded to show me exactly how he came upon this interdimensional glimpse that belonged to both of us, by asking me to stand where he had been standing while we were practicing, and directing me to peripherally gaze at the mirror.

What I saw was the reflection of the curtain in the room with sunlight shining through it. As I kept on looking, my peripheral vision came into focus and the scene of the flickering lights appeared, not in the mirror but on my right side, as if the fire was still burning at that moment!

I was flooded with questions at the end of the session. After this experience I became a true enigma, even to myself.

How could I be there, in Tibet, in another time continuum, doing Dragon's Tears *with Lujan, and simultaneously be here, on an island in Thailand, learning what Lujan calls shamanism?*

The question begged to be answered: Who am I really? And how can that past life feel like it is still happening?

This spontaneous event gives a clear example of how the present moment continuum releases pertinent information when we avail ourselves to the mysteriousness of that moment that is continually escaping us.

What manifested related to a time-space continuum that had previously taken place, around two hundred and sixty years ago, wherein I was teaching my student this movement form in Tibet. The influx of information had to do with the fact that we were both empty enough to receive our symbiotic memory.

The whole sequence was absolutely recognizable via the fact that the déjà vu was realized by the two of us simultaneously. The social paradigm that surrounds talking was replaced by an act of seeing.

This is why it is so vitally important to communicate what you become aware of and finally relinquish your socially bound attention, so that the true manifestation of Spirit can intervene; not by our request but on our behalf.

Eternity communicates with us because we are it and it is us. Awakening our potential increasingly avails us to these omens. We must develop our full capacity to recognize when and how the unknown presents itself to us, and this has very much to do with letting go of what you socially expect.

Gestures externally manifest yet are internally revealed, through our primal ability to recognize the true feelings that arise as a symbiotic happening, to witness and receive as insight.

When you understand that these gestures are of you and for you, you begin to see the *not-doing*s of your internal and external self, communicating as an all-pervading omnipresence. Then you will become aware of being interdimensionally connected to an enormous grid.

To fully understand assimilating this ultimate recapitulation within our body consciousness, we must go to the next seven gates of dreaming awake and resolve with these techniques how to deal with the bioelectric pressure that arises from within.

There is no thought.

There is only realization.

The Last Seven Gates

I'd like you to concentrate very strongly now, yet softly peruse your internal awareness. When you listen to what you can't hear, what will appear for you is profound: An enormity, a great silence.

From here, you will entrain your awareness to ride upon the silent breath and fully focus your attention on your skin. This is your second gate.

Imagine for one moment that your skin carries upon its

essence gestures and not words. If you apply words, they become interference. Even simply saying "skin" imposes a barrier to your experience.

When someone touches your hand, you don't think, "Someone is touching me." You have the realization that you're being touched, and it isn't attached to a word, it's connected to a gesture. Without thought, your eyes automatically view that embrace. Then they travel from the hand to the eyes of the person.

These are full gestures. You know what is held within it them, the feeling is transmitted. Whether the touch itself is simple or complex, the gesture is always obvious.

There is no thought. There is only realization. This is the way that you must travel through the next seven gates, as a gesture to yourself.

Now you have your attention on your skin. Your eyes are closed and you're very relaxed. Always do it like this first, calm and relaxed.

The largest receptor you have is your skin. It surrounds you, and its function is to be aware. When listening to what you can't hear and focusing your eyes inwardly, you peruse the feeling that is your skin. It covers you. It contains you.

Breathe deeply into your lower abdomen, pushing your diaphragm down gently as you listen to what you can't hear, and become sensitive to the feeling that you obtain through being aware of your skin. It's magnetic. It's electric.

Remember when I showed you how to lower your hands when you had your eyes closed, and you felt the magnetism appear in the palms of your hands?

What I'd like you to do is to repeat this process again. Lift your hands and lower them very, very slowly, with your eyes closed, so you can obtain the sensation, the feeling of magnetism, and be fully aware of your skin in the area of your hands.

As you follow the feelings of your skin by listening to what you can't hear, you watch what you're feeling.

While practicing this exercise your eyes touch upon the sensation. You realize you're contained. You can see within and feel what surrounds you. There's only a slight barrier, which is your skin, presenting itself to you.

Once you're there, concentrate on the feeling of your small capillaries that are located underneath your skin. Here is the third gate.

What will happen is that the vibratory essence or the energy of your skin will then dive more deeply into your body. You enter into your capillaries, the small blood vessels which feed your skin.

Before, you were sensing your skin radiating outwardly. Now your awareness is traversing inwardly. You have become aware of the capillaries.

These capillaries feel different from your skin because

they're underneath it. You've dropped or fallen beneath the gate of your skin.

As you become aware of your capillaries, you will notice there is a subtle difference between the first sensation, of the skin, and the second, of the capillaries.

From your capillaries, you then go to your nerve endings, the fourth gate. Once you arrive upon your nerve endings, you'll feel small pinpricks everywhere, electrical locations. As you feel these electrical pinpricks, you realize that you've gone deeper.

You're nestled within the same area of your capillaries, yet the nerve endings give you a different feeling. You go deeper into that feeling, sinking into these nerve endings. Once you feel that, then you've obtained the electrical impulse that comes from your nerve endings.

If you can't feel it everywhere at once in the beginning, commence by focusing on your hands and the bottom of your feet. It's a matter of learning to recognize it. You don't need to force anything. Once you perceive that there are hundreds of locations on your hands, then you've discovered your nerve endings.

From your nerve endings, you travel toward your large arteries. This is the fifth gate. The way you arrive upon this powerful location is that you focus on the center of your body.

You go down to your groin or underneath your arms, and you can feel the pressure of your large arteries pushing the blood through these areas, or alternatively you can locate that pulsation somewhere in your upper torso.

When you feel the sensation of throbbing, you know you've arrived at your arteries. Breathe deeply and experience the pulsation of these arterial channels emanating throughout your body. You might even feel them a little bit under your ears. You never know where the feeling is going to lead you. You go where it makes itself available.

Once you are there, you have arrived at a very powerful gate. You've gone very deeply into the center of your body. As you breathe harmoniously, you compress your breath into your lower abdomen.

While you're listening to what you can't hear, you watch what you can't see and you touch what you really can't locate, yet it is all identifiable through your concentration.

From your arteries, you expand to your bones, the sixth gate. As you expand to your bones, you feel the large arteries connecting to them.

You breathe in, compressing your diaphragm down, and you obtain a connection between your arteries and your bones. This is the ancient art of bone marrow breathing.

The best way to discover where your bones are is to tap your shin and proceed with your meditation. Once you connect with that feeling of density, you may go to your shin or anywhere in your bones that your awareness directs you to.

Breathe from your arteries to your bones.

As you breathe in, become aware of your skeletal structure within its entirety. You can travel to any location by merely observing whichever joint or bone you wish to focus upon.

From your teeth to your toes, everything will become available to you. Breathe very deeply into your arteries, and back into your bones. They are intimately connected.

This is one of the most important gates to be in. As you breathe into your bones, you realize that they're breathing in and out of their own volition, in synchronicity with your breath. This is the gate where I would like you to stay the longest. It is the most potent gate for healing, and to support immunity.

From your bones, you expand naturally to your musculature, the seventh gate. All your muscles become softly obvious to you. All of a sudden, you feel like something has bloomed inside of you, since you've moved from the feeling of your bones and you're now fully within your musculature.

This expanding feeling that you have obtained is the sensation of your musculature making itself available, yet somehow you simultaneously disappear from yourself.

Now we must move very quickly to the eighth gate: Your heart. Once you arrive there, you become aware of its persistent throbbing. You watch its vitality. This gate contains the strongest photonic charge, and the most powerful field of energy that is within you.

You become aligned with your heart's pulsation and its beating. You attempt to listen to it as you watch it. You feel it even though you're not touching it. You breathe deeply in and out. Your eyes and feeling are anchored within your breath, observing this location. This is the last gate.

What we do at the last gate is very special. As you watch your heart beating, you have become very deeply immersed within. As you watch this ever-present organ, fall behind its pulsations with a sense of yourself floating into an omnipresent darkness, a void-like substance behind your heart.

As you gradually descend harmoniously into this reservoir, you realize that the feeling is contained, and the beating that was there becomes less obvious and disappears by virtue of falling behind that precious gate.

As you descend into this blackness, you realize that you can't really locate your heart. Its rhythmic beating becomes so soft that it is hard to identify. As you arrive at the deepest point of the eighth gate, you locate a very beautiful space of silence.

There are three things that can occur when you arrive there. You may see a flash of light, swirling colors, or an image.

Once you are behind your eighth gate and you are settled in there, if you have any of the three experiences described —

for example if you see a flash of light — immediately return to the sensation of your skin and start the whole process all over again. This must equally be applied with colors or imagery, until the void exists within the deepest reservoirs of yourself.

This cannot be emphasized enough, the importance of absolutely emptying oneself. It is vital that you look at and feel the sensation of your skin.

Don't think the word *skin*. Don't think upon any of the gates. You must look at them, realize them, and feel them. You must never talk to yourself about them, for thought does not belong in your body.

To reiterate, whenever you get a flash of light, an image or some color, you go back to your skin, and you traverse your gates once again.

From your skin to your capillaries, from your capillaries to your nerve endings, from your nerve endings to your arteries, from your arteries to your bones, from your bones to your muscle, from your musculature to your heart.

From your heart, you become immersed within the void. This is where your eighth gate leads you, to that omnipresence within. In actuality it is very similar to falling asleep, yet you are fully aware of what you are doing.

When you fall behind your heart into blackness, you wait for something to happen. You'll never hear anything; you'll always see color, or an image, or light. When any of these things occur then you automatically go back to your skin again and start the whole process once more.

You look at your skin, you feel your skin, you listen to your skin. You don't say the word. Words don't belong in this area of consciousness.

Be with your skin. Be with your capillaries. Be with your nerve endings. Be with your arteries. Be with your bones. Be with your musculature. Be with your heart and fall behind your heart again. You can repeat this whole process for as long as your body wants you to. Learn to listen to it.

It is only necessary to stay at each gate for as long as it gives its sensation to you. The power of that gate will command you to move upon the withdrawal of its sensation from your consciousness.

You must move from each gate and realize that it is commanding you to proceed to the next gate by disappearing or becoming less obvious to your internal gaze that is listening to and feeling the process that is occurring. Its withdrawal from you indicates that you are harmoniously proceeding to your next port of call, your next destination.

At some point within this awakened meditation you will find that you are in your eighth gate, falling into the omnipresent enormity of that blackness, and nothing presents itself to you for five of ten minutes.

Nothing's there and you are stable. You're watching your breath. You're listening to what you can't see. You're watching what you can't feel. The intangible becomes obvious to you. You're full of emptiness, and emptiness is full within you.

If no phenomenon occurs, no pictures, no light, no color, then breathe deeply and quietly, gently compressing your diaphragm into your abdomen. This is the region known as the lower dantien, three of four digits below the navel into the center of the body. For a woman, this is also the area of the womb.

Here we find a non-locatable zone of emptiness that can only be sensed and is similar to the space that's behind your heart, which is your middle dantien. Now you have arrived at your prenatal essence.

You're breathing very quietly and very deeply. You locate this central matrix via the electrical pulsation that travels along the pathway of your aortic arteries.

As you detect the pulsation, cup your left hand just above your pubic bone, with your little finger resting against your lower abdomen. Then place your right hand above your left hand, resting on the skin, with your right palm facing up and your two thumbs touching together in the center, sitting like a Buddha.

Focus on your lower dantien until you pinpoint the electrical impulse that corresponds with the beating of your heart that travels along your arterial pathways to be pooled within this location.

As the sensation increases, the electromagnetism from your lower dantien merges with the pulsation and electricity of your hands. The beating of your heart becomes a softness, a thrumming that connects your entire organism.

As you sit there, you begin to become very magnetic, empty yet simultaneously full. This empty fullness expands from your lower dantien to encompass your whole body.

You feel very comfortable within the act of observation, observing that which you can't see, feeling that which you can't really touch; yet it's made itself available to you, through listening to what you can't hear.

You only have one chance,

and it lasts a lifetime.

Your Photonic Potential

Through the gateway of your heart, you will enter into your intangible self. From that vantage point you wait for an indication of what to take from your center to the outskirts of your physical being, your skin, and from there you begin to travel once again towards your heart.

The reason why you do this is that all of your photonic potential is rippling from within, outwardly toward your surface. You journey to the fullest boundary of yourself externally, then you dive back in.

Never returning to your internal dialogue, you allow the natural emanation of your photonic potential to stay within, as an expression of your body consciousness, never of your mind. Your silent command center is then reinstated through this process.

Remember that everything that occurs during the last seven gates is an experience to be witnessed; it is a process of observing what you are interfering with rather than interfering with what you are observing.

Everything will appear as it is, while you witness what was, which then becomes what is. If nothing appears within the void-like expanse behind your heart, then dive more deeply into that darkness, that cosmic consciousness.

Slowly and harmoniously descend to your lower dantien and collect the magnetism that is inherently there, awaiting to be rediscovered. Collect the full potential of yourself there, within silence.

I want you to know that the inescapable will never escape you once you realize it. What you're doing is training yourself to be within emptiness and simultaneously within form. There is no need to subject yourself to experiencing this as a contradiction. Disappear from that. Disappear from yourself.

Seeing

For those of you who want to see, it is vitally important to realize that for you to progress on your path, you need to stop thinking. The external anomaly known as the holographic image, which appears as composites of sensory data to be assimilated by the seer, will not occur if thought is present.

The reason for this is that the resonant field connected to thinking is incompatible with seeing. Thought destroys the delicate membrane that surrounds the holographic image, which neutralizes that event as a result of the incapacity of these two frequencies to harmoniously interact.

Another way to elucidate this delicate impasse is that thought collapses the wave function of the holographic image, which is omnipresently communicated as a gesture of spirit.

In other words, if you think, you won't see. And if you see, you can't think.

When subtleties become substance,

wisdom arrives.

Eight Gates Summary

By practicing the *Eight Gates* you will naturally arrive into a state of being, knowing, and *not-doing*. Enter these portals with the awareness that your body will direct you exactly where you need to be. Thought cannot accompany you on this journey.

Your doing becomes the action that you watch, which transforms into the feeling that you traverse. This vibration delivers you into a state of being that then reveals to you what you know, in connection with how your body feels or interacts with you.

Your receptivity is a gesture of acquiescence that is subtly echoed back to you. Even though you are your body, it nevertheless speaks to you. It asks of you to be kinesthetically aware, yet empty within that center.

When your attention examines your body consciousness by watching the sensations that arise, your physical response will be exacting in terms of directives supplied towards your being.

Don't make the mistake of speaking to yourself as you do this. An internal verbal decree will not yield the awareness you are seeking. Only the feeling gives you a point of arrival.

You know you're at your nerve endings when you feel the hundreds of pinpricks. The sensation tells you. You learn to view your body and watch it from within, with the internal viewing capacity of your eyes that travels upon your silent breath, listening intently to what arises as your two percent cursory glance guards your periphery. Via this process your attention becomes a *not-doing* of your very beingness. This is the essence of the *Eight Gates*.

This sacred practice is a complete recapitulation of the moment that you exist in that is continually escaping you, for it gives pause.

That circumstance is your life path and as it stops you in your tracks you discover who you are. Then you can make really valuable choices about what you need to do next, and by virtue of this resolve become of service to the planet.

This is the most important step for all of us to take now, to discover what is valuable to this world, and truly educate ourselves about that.

Wisdom reveals itself through the act of watching what you can't see, listening to what you can't hear, and feeling that which can't be touched.

Eight Gates Summary

Remember, if you're in a state of being and you begin to enter into knowing and doing, you've taken that deleterious fourth step towards the internal nagging that will justify, through its own reflective process, a cloaked phylum whose repetitive semantic insertions willfully propel one's life force away from our most precious resource: Introspective silence.

Realize that it is not the power of your thoughts that has value. It is your gestures that signify who you really are. Whatever is taking place internally will radiate from its source and meet the world on the level of feeling.

A negative thought process becomes an abusive gesture that makes the presence of a person harboring this vibration untenable.

Such reverberations emanate in the same way with an individual who is non-invasive, only they practice not being there, so the effect may come across as completely alien in comparison to the social paradigm that most of us are immersed within at this moment in time. So much so that most will not even detect the unassuming approach of an earthling practicing these principles. When emptiness is embraced, one's omnipresence becomes available.

Be a light unto yourself,

thus illuminating everything else.

General Esoterics

I would like to add two more elements that will illuminate different areas of the practice of the *Eight Gates*, honoring their origins through this gesture.

I will further expand upon the general esoteric principles of *Lo Ban Pai*, specifically in relation to the method of bone marrow breathing and the true microcosmic orbit, which I will fully introduce in the next chapter. Both of these techniques are substantially different to everything that is being taught presently under these names.

Bone marrow breathing is part of the *Eight Gates*, and when you follow the sequence of instructions presented you will arrive upon this practice naturally and without struggle.

When the large arteries are focused on, they illuminate the skeletal structure to be viewed from within. As this occurs you may notice that your attention is alerted to identify a place that needs your focus.

When your perception locates this area via the pulsations from your arterial cortex, your eyes will automatically witness that silent command from within.

It is important to know that once you have identified an area — say, your left knee — for observation in terms of healing, it is vital to bring symmetry to your awareness by allowing your attention to find exactly the same area on the other side.

Once your perception is balanced in this way, the arteries

will naturally pulsate more strongly, delivering blood and chi to each location equally. If this practice within bone marrow breathing is not applied, then the power of the arterial cortex will not be activated correctly.

For example, if your left hip is painful, focus on the opposite hip to stimulate the blood flow and chi to identify and connect with every bone in your body.

The pulsations emanating from the arteries accompany the bones to the outer reaches of your physicality — the fingertips, toes, top of the head and perineum — and through this process these pathways are illuminated, thus allowing the practitioner to identify the sensations of the macrocosmic orbit within the confines of the human form.

Practicing this enables your consciousness to recognize the source of your internal energy, flowing harmoniously through the centers of your lower, middle and upper dantien simultaneously, thus opening up the central circuit of *Jing Chi Shen* to be witnessed.

Jing is connected to your lower dantien, *Chi* is connected to your middle dantien, which is located at the level of your heart center, and *Shen* is connected to the upper dantien, at your third eye region. Each of these centers have vibratory, sensory elements within their unique structure and are absolutely interconnected.

There are a few identifiable points in the third eye that may make themselves obvious to the initiate when practicing. The first area may be felt one digit above the bridge of the nose, and pulsations will be experienced an inch inside the cranial cavity, which causes a pressure and spinning that may activate a sensation that feels like your ears are gently thrumming.

Simultaneously the area of the forehead will manifest a rotational eddy that resembles a spinning vortex, as though there is pressure being applied to the mid-eyebrow region.

When this occurs, two channels may become apparent within your awareness. These are internally located, flowing down the right and left hand sides of the central channel of the body and culminating at the lower dantien, where they meet and ascend centrally to the upper dantien, flowing through the fontanel, and cascade toward the kidney points on the bottom of the feet; giving a sensation of rooting to the ground whilst connecting to the heavens via the crown chakra.

If you are fortunate enough to perceive them, you will experience an overwhelming joy welling up within your body.

The second phenomenon that may occur is that one's perception can become externally located, for example, by seeing a blue or indigo sphere appearing outside of the mid-eyebrow region.

A third sensation that may arise is a pulsating awareness that appears at the tip of the nose. Here the energy naturally drops, silently flowing down towards the perineal region, so as to relocate the practitioner within the lower dantien.

These are a few of the experiences that you may obtain

by practicing bone marrow breathing in the Eight Gates. Similar sensations, or even the same ones, will occur when you access your microcosmic orbit correctly.

During your practice — when sitting comfortably, whether upright in full lotus, lounging backwards on a couch, or sitting in a chair — notice that your tongue is touching the top of your palette by virtue of the fact that your lips are gently closed.

Be aware that you should never clench your teeth. Let your jaw drop naturally. You may experience your teeth touching or not. It doesn't matter, as long as your tongue is gently embracing the upper palette and the lips are properly sealed.

It is best to have your eyes closed in the beginning, to gather your ninety-eight percent within, so that your ears become externally bound, thus providing the two percent of your attention with the expansive reach that your external auditory function provides.

The next step is to be aware not to tighten or clamp your perineum to the point where it becomes locked. Let it sit naturally. In other words, don't try. Let it be.

It is important to realize that all of these elements must be gently applied within the *Eight Gates, Bone Marrow Breathing*, and the *Microcosmic Orbit*.

If your anal floor is prolapsed in any way whatsoever, you can sit up in a chair and place a squash ball in this region. Being seated upright in this manner will facilitate sealing this area via the downward pressure applied.

The ball should not touch the skin, so as to prevent absorption of any foreign residues in this very sensitive area. It is noteworthy to mention here another technique regarding locking the perineum.

When you sneeze or cough, retract the anal or perineal floor tightly to lock it. This will avoid any further prolapse. Even for a healthy person it is wise to apply this technique when sneezing or coughing so as to avoid loss of energy or vital chi from this location.

I would also suggest that the perineum is pulled up and locked as part of a separate practice, as in *Kegeling**, to tonify and strengthen this region, in turn increasing the bone density of the hips.

It is difficult to give comprehensive information within a book on this subject, due to the inevitable differences in each individual's physical disposition. The deeper instructions relating to these practices I must reserve for private tuition. Absolutism in this area is impossible to apply in a static format such as written material.

The Eight Gates are usually given in conjunction with the movements of *Lo Ban Pai* that open the channels

---

* Kegel is the exercise of cutting off the flow of urine by pulling up the perineum tightly and then releasing. This is practiced repeatedly to strengthen the sphincter and perineal musculature and has innumerable benefits.

appropriately, so as to resolve any disharmony that may appear or be present within one's physicality.

At the center of your being

there is an answer.

The Microcosmic Orbit

In a time long forgotten, high in the Altai mountains, where shamanism was birthed, a monastery silently stood. A traveller, coming upon the entrance to this remote place, tapped gently upon the threshold and awaited patiently to be received. The monastery door slowly opened and an old monk appeared.

"If you wish to enter the inner sanctum of this temple," he said, you must perform one feat. I will instruct you in the ancient technique of following your internal orbit to open up the gate to the power that lies within you.

"Doing this will allow you to awaken to your full potential, so you may recognize how to proceed with the knowledge that will be forthcoming beyond that point."

Days, weeks and months went by, as the old monk taught the initiate this very special technique. Upon completion of his instruction, he said:

"When you have fully integrated what you are being taught, you must sit outside and melt the snow around your body, one foot in diameter. Then you may gain entry into the deeper facets of yourself, through the teachings that I will impart to you if you succeed in this task."

This is the instruction the old monk gave.

As you are immersed deeply within your inner silence, fall behind the gate of your heart, into a void-like expanse. From there you will drop gently into the center of the lower dantien. Visualize now the feeling of that which you can't see, by touching upon the magnetism that becomes available to you.

Connect your hands and your lower dantien with your primordial chi. Follow that pulsation to the center of your cauldron. See within that deep quietude a shining ember, a red-hot coal from a fire. Know it to be the size of a golf ball.

Become immersed in the fact that it is warm and expansive, even though it is small and compressed. Allow this heat to emanate from within, to the extremities of your luminous cocoon, your energy bubble. See a gentle, red, diffused light embracing you.

Become aware of how your electromagnetic power pulsates within your hands and your lower dantien simultaneously. The red coal provides energy to heat your lower cauldron with a nurturing warmth that goes beyond the boundaries of your physical form to extend and expand to over twelve or thirteen feet in diameter.

Be aware of your arterial cortex pulsating from your lower dantien to your kidneys. Know that they are being strengthened through this act.

As your kidneys are filled with the power of your chi, be aware that the energy is flowing upwards to the back of your neck, pulsating underneath your ears, rising up to your crown and immediately flowing to your third eye cavity, wherever it is located for you, either at the bridge of your nose or two digits above.

At this point you may see a luminous ball outside your mid-eyebrow region, which you have identified through feeling, or a small glowing sphere within your cranial cavity, the size of a golf ball, that will be blue or indigo.

When locating this area you will feel a spinning sensation. Allow yourself to be held there for the time that your power permits.

When the color of your third eye dantien diminishes,

allow your awareness to return to your lower dantien, and then commence the exercise once more. Repeat this instruction until your body requires you to stop.

Your microcosmic orbit, which is the energy running up your spine and down your front, is always operational, as is the macrocosmic orbit.

Be aware that you are becoming acquainted with your full potential via these practices. Feel your tongue upon your upper palette, as your lips are gently closed.

Allow yourself to be sensitive to all of the sensations that arise. Feeling nurtured and whole, return to your dantien to re-establish yourself within the stronghold of that electromagnetic cauldron.

If you wish to increase your strength and resilience, stay within that center, sensing the diffused emanations flowing to your luminous extremities, whilst simultaneously feeling the pulsations of your dantien emanating to your kidneys and your hands as one.

This meditation will help you to become physically robust and energetically capable beyond your current imaginings. When completing any of these exercises, lay down and relax before recommencing your daily activities.

Glossary

To allow everyone the possibility to better understand terminology that may be new or unfamiliar, I will outline here some of the key esoteric terms applied throughout the text.

GLOSSARY

Dantien

The *dantien* is an etheric container and is often referred to as a cauldron. This is due to the fact that all of the elements of our internal alchemy converge and combine within these vital centers, thus feeding the chakras, which, in combination with the dantien, supply the power of energy distribution to the meridian system.

Dantien are found in three locations in the human body, all centrally located. The lower dantien is three digits below the navel within the region of the lower abdomen. The middle dantien is situated at the location of the heart chakra, and the upper dantien is stationed at the mid-eyebrow point.

The location of the upper dantien can vary from person to person, either at the bridge of the nose or one or two digits above this area.

GLOSSARY

Ting Jing

Ting Jing is the power to listen with all of the senses, as has been thoroughly elucidated throughout this whole book.

Fa Jing

Fa Jing is the capacity to issue or discharge power explosively, both at close range and from a distance, as a telekinetic skill.

The Three Treasures: Jing, Chi and Shen

The Three Treasures: *Jing*, *Chi* and *Shen*, are the vital essences located in the lower, middle and upper dantiens.

Jing

Jing is the primal essence or life force that we have inherited from our parents. Jing gives us our physical strength and the power of our will, which is electrically transferred to the heart

GLOSSARY

and the third eye, empowering the capacity of our eyes to see clearly, both from a linear perspective, and interdimensionally.

We only have a limited amount of Jing, which is assigned to us at birth, and when it is depleted, our life ends. Jing is stored in the lower dantien and this is where the power of the kidney essence resides. It is also connected to sexual energy and the production of bone marrow.

CHI

Chi is a universal force that is concentrated within the heart center, or middle dantien. This bioelectric current runs in and throughout the human organism as energetic impulses that can be felt as magnetism.

Chi emanates and extends from the luminous cocoon as frequencies that are sent and received. It is the vital essence that allows the heart center to interpret and communicate within the parameters of its purity, which is reflected as truth.

Chi, in combination with the breath, animates

harmonious movement in and throughout the human biofield, allowing our organs to function optimally to disseminate vital essence and to facilitate the smooth flow of blood.

Shen

Shen is a form of energy that emanates from the mid eyebrow, and is most active in the very young and in empathic seers. It is essentially the light that shines behind a person's eyes, giving the ability to see beyond the manifest universe.

When Shen is strong it gives the power to perceive the holographic structure of the cosmos itself, in the form of frequencies, much in the same way as a whale or dolphin sends and receives sound waves using sonar.

This receptivity allows them to identify and gather data regarding the essential blueprint of their surroundings, for assimilation and dissemination amongst their kind.

We receive and transmit information in much the same way, via our third eye center, where Shen is located. The third eye, in combination with our heart, is connected to our interdimensional capacity to perceive the vast ocean of awareness that we are absolutely immersed within.

It is noteworthy at this point to mention that the third eye and the heart chakra are vibrationally paired to interpret feeling and imagery simultaneously.

To increase understanding of the function of these vital centers and their relationship to one another, you can imagine your body consciousness as a light unto itself: a lamp. The Jing is the vital fuel that sustains the Chi as a constant flame, thus allowing the radiant light of Shen to illuminate the omnipresent darkness.

Never forget what you are meant to remember.

Don't even think about it.

For information regarding workshops
and private tuition with Lujan Matus please visit:
www.parallelperception.com

Printed in Great Britain
by Amazon